Out of Control

Finding Hope in a Broken World

Rodney Hunt

WESTBOW
PRESS®
A DIVISION OF THOMAS NELSON
& ZONDERVAN

WestBow Press books may be ordered through booksellers or by contacting:

WestBow Press
A Division of Thomas Nelson & Zondervan
1663 Liberty Drive
Bloomington, IN 47403
www.westbowpress.com
1 (866) 928-1240

ISBN: 978-1-5127-6011-8 (sc)
ISBN: 978-1-5127-6490-1 (hc)
ISBN: 978-1-5127-6012-5 (e)

Library of Congress Control Number: 2016916866

Print information available on the last page.

WestBow Press rev. date: 11/28/2016

Contents

Acknowledgements

I want to thank all of my encouragers. You have lifted my spirits, and it was often your timely words that gave me the encouragement to continue this work even when I felt like giving up. Ronda, you have encouraged me throughout the process of writing this book, but more importantly, you have encouraged me continuously throughout our lives together. You are my cheerleader and always offer words of affirmation to me. You gave me feedback on the content of this book over and over. You endured many hours of me sitting in my chair in the living room as I wrote this book while neglecting other chores around the house. Thank you for understanding and being so supportive! You are the love of my life!

I want to thank my assistant, Carole Wells, who bought me a typewriter that I keep in my office. It has helped remind me of the calling to write. You also encouraged me to begin this book with the three opening stories I share.

Steve Pharr, thank you for your constant encouragement throughout this process. You kept me inspired to finish the work every time you popped into my office and said, "#1 Best Seller." You are a great friend.

Mark Cundiff, your words of encouragement also helped me keep going when I was at a point where I couldn't see the light at the end of the tunnel. Thank you!

Jeff Brewer, it was your words of encouragement that helped me begin this project. You have a knack for speaking words of wisdom to me at the right time.

Thank you to my editors and proofreaders! Melissa Arnold, Carole Wells, Robin Christian, Rebecca Lindsey, Laci Post, Theresa Anderson, Kathy Schillo, Maryanne Abbate, and Sheila Harris caught many grammatical errors in my work and helped me identify powerful parts of my book. Each of you endured the tough task of plowing through an unfinished work. I appreciate all the time you gave to read and make suggestions.

A special thank you to Lauren Eckert for doing the final edit and proofreading on such short notice! I appreciate all your work and effort to help me get my book to its final version.

I want to thank Brian Bloye, Paul Richardson, and Steve Veale, who have had a huge impact on my life and ministry through their friendship, teaching, and the way they passionately follow Jesus. Brian, thank you for your pioneering spirit and obedience to God's call to plant West Ridge Church. A special thank you to Matt Wilmington, who was instrumental in bringing me on staff full-time in 2006. West Ridge has been a place for me and my family to worship, serve, and work. Next to heaven, West Ridge has always been like home for me. We have seen God do some incredible things here in northwest Atlanta and around the world!

Although I have never met him, I would like to thank Dr. Wayne Grudem for his teaching and ministry. Dr. Grudem's *Systematic Theology* has been an incredible resource for me in writing this book and throughout my ministry. Also, the ESV Study Bible has helped me tremendously over the years in my personal study of the Scriptures. Thank you for your devotion to the study and explanation of the Scriptures!

Finally, thank you to Annie Downs who helped me get started on this journey and who introduced me to WestBow Press!

Introduction

EXPERIENCING BROKENNESS

Christopher and Jamie Lynn Sparkman

On the morning of April 29, 2014, a disturbed, 19-year-old man entered a shipping facility in Kennesaw, Georgia. The gunman wore black clothes, a camouflage vest, a shoulder ammo belt, a knife, and a shotgun. He had one intent that day - to kill. Before he came to the facility, he wrote a final note: "I'm a sociopath. I want to hurt people. This is not anyone's fault but mine."[1]

As he entered the facility, the first person standing in his path was Christopher Sparkman. Christopher was employed as a security guard by a local security company. He picked up a second shift that day to earn some extra money. It was a few minutes before his shift ended. Soon he would go home to his wife. They would be celebrating their one-year anniversary in a few weeks. Christopher's replacement was right beside him, ready to take over.

The gunman entered the building and began shooting. Christopher took the first shotgun blast at point-blank range in the abdomen. The pellets pierced Christopher's body and internal organs. He was the first of six victims shot that day and was the most seriously wounded.

As Christopher lay on the floor, wounded from the blast, he thought of others before himself. Somehow, he managed to call 911. "I've been shot," Christopher told the dispatcher. "Please tell my wife I love her. I'm losing energy really fast."

The dispatcher repeatedly told Christopher, "Stay on the line with me. Don't hang up."[2]

I met Christopher and his wife Jamie Lynn a little over a year before that day for several sessions of premarital counseling. I liked them. I could tell they complimented each other well. I felt they were a good match for each other.

In one of the premarital sessions with Christopher and Jamie Lynn, I told them, as I tell most couples, that marriage takes more than love. It also takes faith. It takes faith because you don't know what the future holds. There are no guarantees. There is no crystal ball to look into. Marriage involves risk.

They understood this. Both said they were ready to face the future together. I agreed, and they were married May 25, 2013. Even though I had told them that marriage took faith, I never dreamed that their faith would be tested in such a dramatic way so soon.

Christopher and Jamie Lynn on their wedding day.

It was apparent to me that Christopher was the kind of guy who would lay down his life, if necessary, to protect his wife, family, or country. He had already proved that by serving in the U.S. Army, where he was stationed in Kuwait as a traffic controller for 10 months. I knew he was the type of man who would do whatever it took to show his love for his wife. I had no idea he would end up sacrificing himself in order to protect those who worked at the shipping facility that day.

As fate would have it, a package handler trainer who used to be an emergency medical technician was working at the facility on the day of the shooting. As he rushed to Christopher's aid, his former training and experience prepared him to be able to help Christopher. He held pressure on the wound from the shotgun blast until an ambulance arrived.

The former emergency medical technician later told a reporter, "God put me in the right place at the right time. That's all Him. He's the only reason I got out of there today."[3]

Even in the midst of a terrible tragedy, you can find traces of God's provision.

Christopher was rushed to the hospital, where surgeons operated for hours to save his life.

After I received the call that Christopher had been shot, I drove to the hospital to be with his family. I sat in the waiting room with family members in disbelief over what had happened. We prayed for Christopher. We did not know then if he would live or die.

The surgeon worked tirelessly as we prayed through many hours of surgery. By the grace of God and the work of some very skilled surgeons, Christopher survived this brutal attack. He would face a long journey of recovery, a journey that he is still on to this day.

Since the shooting, he's experienced over 50 surgeries in the past two years trying to repair the damage from that blast and has spent over 300 days in the hospital. Jamie Lynn has been right there by his side, day and night, acting as a nurse, caretaker, and wife.

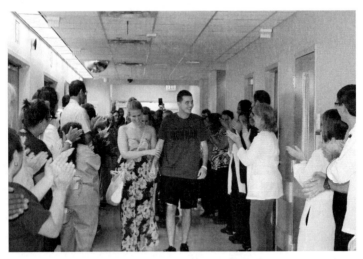

Christopher getting to go home from the hospital- July 4, 2014.

In one of my early visits to the hospital while Christopher was still in ICU, he pointed out a Bible verse that his wife had placed on a board

4

directly in front of his hospital bed. It read, "You intended to harm me, but God intended it all for good. He brought me to this position so I could save the lives of many people" (Genesis 50:12 NLT). In the midst of pain and uncertainty about his future, Christopher had faith and hope.

He and Jamie Lynn choose to cling to the promise that God is in control. They choose to forgive the gunman who almost took Christopher's life. They believe that God can bring good out of this situation, even though someone else had intended to harm them. Although they are still going through many difficult days that test their faith, they hold fast to the promise that God has plans to give them a hope and a future. I believe this, too.

Randy and Sharon Flowers

On a Sunday night in September 2012, I was reminded how quickly life can change. We had just celebrated our church's 15th anniversary that evening with outdoor picnics and a fireworks show. I was tired after a full day of work and went to bed early.

My wife, Ronda, came in to wake me up sometime between 12:30 and 1:00 a.m. on Monday. Barely awake, I could hear the concern in her voice. Something was wrong. She said, "I have to go to the hospital. Something is wrong with Sharon!" Her brother, Randy, had called from an ambulance moments earlier. He was now with the paramedics in the ambulance as they were working on Sharon. As the sirens blared in the background, Ronda knew from her brother's voice that this was serious. Ronda said Sharon couldn't breathe and they were on their way to the hospital.

Sharon Flowers at Cape San Blas in June of 2009.

At the age of 46, Sharon really didn't have any major health issues. She didn't take any medications. She didn't drink, smoke, or do anything that would cause her to stop breathing all of a sudden. I couldn't imagine what was wrong. I told Ronda I was sure she would be OK.

"I have to leave and go be at the hospital with Randy," she said. I agreed. Nothing would have kept Ronda from rushing to the hospital to be with her brother and sister-in-law.

Both of our girls were in bed asleep. I told Ronda I would stay home with the kids while she went. I laid back in the bed. But there was no way I could go back to sleep. I began to pray.

I waited anxiously to hear back from my wife. It wasn't much later that she texted me. The message was, "She is gone."

I texted her back, "What do you mean, she is gone? Gone from the hospital?"

"No," my wife said. "She passed away." I was in shock. It didn't seem real. There must be a mistake. This couldn't be happening.

It all happened so suddenly, without warning. Why? How? It couldn't be.

I thought of her three children growing up without their mom. I thought of my brother-in-law being a single dad and raising the kids by himself. I thought of how just a year before, Randy and Ronda's dad had also died unexpectedly on a Sunday night in September. Randy had lost both his wife and his father in a year's time. My wife had lost her dad and sister-in-law (one of her best friends for over 25 years) in a year's time.

The reality is that, at some point, if it hasn't already, this out-of-control world will become personal for you. It will visit your doorstep. It is much like an unwelcome guest who shows up unexpectedly to the door of your life.

It doesn't call ahead. It simply kicks the door down. It can crash into your life like a rock through a window, demolishing your carefully laid out plans, leaving shards of shattered expectations laying all over the floor.

How do you find hope in moments like this? It isn't easy, but you can. In the midst of heartache and loss, our family has found hope. I have walked alongside many other families in moments like this and watched them cling to hope. You can, too.

Other times, it is problems with our relationships that throw our world out of control.

Broken Vows

He couldn't remember how he got to this point. He told me there was a woman at work whom he had befriended. What began as

7

a working relationship grew into a close friendship. He began to confide in her. He shared secrets and dreams with her that he hadn't even shared with his wife. He felt safe with her.

Neither had set out to go to this place in their relationship; it just seemed to happen subtly over time. The more they talked, the more he wanted to spend time with her. He looked for excuses to text her, talk to her, and see her.

He felt like she understood him in a way his wife didn't. She was attractive. She affirmed him. Then he did something he never dreamed he would do after marrying the love of his life. It seemed to come naturally for him. He didn't "fall" into this moment. He made small decisions over the course of several months that led to what happened next.

They were alone. His emotions tingled with excitement and anticipation. As he looked into her eyes, he felt a strong connection with her. He leaned toward her and kissed her. While the thrill of emotion surged through his entire body as his lips pressed against hers, he knew it was wrong. But his emotions were stronger than his conscience. He was fulfilling a desire he had felt for her for a while.

Not all of our desires are right. Not all of our desires are wrong. They have to be filtered. Things that are off limits have a way of enticing our self-centered desires. They can be more appealing. They promise immediate benefits. We see it. We want it. But we are blinded to the hook that lies buried deep within. Deceived by our own selfish desires, we take it. As we bite into it, the barbs of the hook rip and tear our heart. There are consequences.

He dealt a blow to his marriage. He had promised his wife 10 years ago in his wedding vows to reserve his physical and emotional intimacy for her alone, to forsake all others. He had said, "I do." By kissing his co-worker, he broke those promises.

Trust is one of the most fragile aspects of the relationship between a husband and wife. It can be easily shattered if it is dishonored. Once trust is lost, it may never be found again.

The truth is, we've all experienced the brokenness of this world: broken dreams, hopes, and expectations. You lose your job. An unexpected circumstance catches you by surprise. Someone you love dies. A relationship fails. You do something you regret. What I want to remind you is that, regardless of your situation, you can find hope in an out-of-control world.

There is hope because God is picking up the pieces of our lives to make us whole again. There is hope because he has a plan. While we will experience pain and loss, God will restore our joy and restore that which has been lost.

That promise is repeated over and over many times in the Scriptures. God will restore. He will pay back. What was lost will be found again. In fact, we will receive much more back than what we lost.

There is a better future than what you are seeing and experiencing right now. You need to know that in a world where so much seems set against you, God is in control, and he is on your side. God is not your enemy. He is your advocate and defender. He wants what is best for you. He wants to give you a future and a hope.

Yet we often must first experience darkness before we can see the light. We have to be lost before we can appreciate the elation of being found. We have to be broken before we can be made whole. We have to die before we can truly live. These are the paradoxes of life on earth.

While we all have the opportunity to find hope, not everyone does. Many miss it. Some reject it. Others wander aimlessly through life. The Scriptures tell us, "There is a path before each person that seems right, but it ends in death" (Proverbs 14:12 NLT). That is a strong statement. I don't want you to go down that path.

The Scriptures say there is a gateway to life where hope can be found. Maybe you are already on that path. Maybe you have grown weary as you've journeyed on that path. Maybe the path has become unclear and you need to be reminded of the many promises of hope and a future God has for you. No matter where you are at and no matter what path you are currently on, you can find meaning and purpose as you understand God's plans for your life.

To begin, we have to understand how we got into this predicament. We have to go back to where it all started. This story sets the context for why bad things happen in our world.

Part 1
WHY ARE THINGS OUT OF CONTROL?

Chapter 1

REBELLION IN HEAVEN

In order to understand why things are out of control, I need to take you back to the beginning.

In the beginning, there was only God and nothing except God. There were no people. There was no time. There was no physical matter. There was just – God. God was content in himself. He didn't need anything or anyone else to complete him. Contrary to the idea of yin and yang, there were no conflicting forces at work - only God. And God was good. Nothing was out of control.

That is hard for us to imagine. We experience a life with things we can see, touch, hear, and smell. There are bills to pay, people to relate with, and places to go. But it wasn't always this way. Before there was anything physical, there was only the spiritual. What we can see came from what we can't see. The Scriptures tell us, "By faith we understand that the entire universe was formed at God's command, that what we now see did not come from anything that can be seen" (Hebrews 11:3 NLT).

That is how what we see came about. God spoke, and with a command, he created all there is, from the tiniest cell to the largest galaxy. "In the beginning God created the heavens and the earth" (Genesis 1:1 NLT). From this one sentence, we find that God created all matter, space, and time. The ground that you walk on, the air that you breathe, and the water that you drink - all of it was made by God.

Everything he made was good. There was no sadness, only joy. There was no discontentment, only peace. There was no death, only life. Nothing was lacking. There was a beautiful rhythm to the way creation worked. Things were "under control."

This is the type of world God created for us. Not one filled with pain, heartache, and death. He didn't want your marriage to struggle. He didn't want you to live with sickness. He didn't want you to struggle with your emotions. God's original intent for you was good, is good, and always will be good. The things that are out of control in your life can cause you to question whether or not God's plans for you are good, but the Scriptures give you assurance that they are good and always have been good, even though it may not seem like it in the moment.

At some point after God created all things good, something happened to bring about the mess we see and experience today. A rebellion happened. Some of the creatures God created turned on him and brought confusion to the order God had established. This rebellion would change the course of history and the fate of our world.

The rebellion began with one of God's most dignified and powerful angels - Satan. Pride entered his heart. His pride said, "I will ascend to heaven and set my throne above God's stars. I will preside on the mountain of the gods far away in the north. I will climb to the highest heavens and be like the Most High" (Isaiah 14:13-14 NLT). [1]

Satan, who was created good, turned evil.

Satan wanted God's place. He wanted to rule. The created wanted the place of the Creator. God gave Satan a role of prominence and power, but that wasn't good enough. He wanted more. He wanted the worship. He wanted all the power. He wanted control. So he rebelled to take what he wanted.

In his rebellion, he led many other angels in an attempted mutiny against God. Angels of light transformed into demons of darkness. Like Satan, they rejected their God-assigned place. Jude writes, "And I remind you of the angels who did not stay within the limits of authority God gave them but left the place where they belonged" (Jude 1:6 NLT).

There must have been a great battle in heaven. Angel against angel. Sword against sword. Will against will as powerful spiritual beings fought. Satan and his followers created havoc in heaven. However, they were no match for God and his angels. They lost the battle and lost their place in heaven.

This power play for control led by Satan was the first step leading to our world being thrown out of control. One of the most powerful angels in God's court turned and created havoc in heaven. The irony is that while he sought to gain control of God's throne and position, he lost control.

---

[1] (*This passage was originally written about the pride of the king of Babylon that led to his fall but has also been interpreted to apply to the pride that led to the fall of Satan.*)

He set out to rob the creation of peace. He became the wolf who snatches up the sheep and scatters them. He became a roaring lion, prowling around looking for someone to devour. He became the great dragon who wages war against the people of earth and the angels in heaven.

He is the originator of all sin. Even though he was created as an angel of great beauty, power, and responsibility to serve God, he turned on God and became God's adversary. In so doing, he also became our adversary.

Satan's sinister threefold plan is to "steal and kill and destroy" (John 10:10 a NLT). That has been his mission throughout the ages and it won't change. He won't repent or change his mind. He seeks to destroy you and all that is good in God's creation.

He is the antagonist in God's story, and he is the antagonist in your story. He is your accuser. The Bible says that he accuses you day and night before God. He continually brings charges against you. He brings up your past sins and your bad choices. He cries out, "Guilty!" in God's court. He is perpetually condemning you. He claims there is nothing good in you. He never stops with his accusations. He is constantly against you and all that is good.

Satan's heavenly rebellion broke the peace that had always existed in heaven. For the first time, there was brokenness in God's created order. These series of events created ripple effects that would go beyond heaven and impact our earthly realm. Although the people on earth didn't know it yet, the actions of these angels, turned demons, would be felt in their world.

Chapter 2

LIVING IN PARADISE

While angels were created with greater power than people, it was men and women who were the crescendo of God's creation. They were created in his own image. "In the image of God he created them; male and female he created them" (Genesis 1:27 NLT).

The uniqueness and distinctiveness of their masculinity and femininity together reflected the image of God. They were royalty. While God was the one in control of all things, he gave some of his authority to both of them. He gave them autonomy and responsibility as his image bearers on earth.

Every person since Adam and Eve has also reflected royalty because we all are created in the image of God. There is intrinsic value in every person. When you look into the face of another human being, male or female, black or white, you are seeing a reflection of who God is and what He is like. People have value not because of what they have done, or can do, but because they are all created in God's image. Understanding this truth affects how we view and treat ourselves and other people. Because you are a descendant of Adam and Eve, you can be assured that you have purpose and a special role in this world. You are designed to reflect the image of your Creator in heaven. You, too, are royalty.

We are the only creatures God made who possess characteristics similar to his. We are able to know and experience love. Communicate. Be in relationship with other people. We are free to make our own choices and decisions. We have power. We can exercise wisdom. We can create. In fact, the creative spark that is in all of us comes from being made in the image of a God who loves to create. Many of the attributes God has are displayed in us to a lesser extent.

Being the first ones created in God's image, Adam and Eve had a unique opportunity that no other person has ever had. They lived in and experienced paradise - Eden. It was a place of luxury and pleasure. It was a place of abundance.

They lived in a place where everything was under control. Adam could work in the garden all day without ever breaking a sweat. He didn't feel any frustration about the work God gave him to do. There was no guilt, no feelings of not measuring up, no sickness, and no death. Every breath of air they breathed in was unpolluted. All of the food they tasted was delicious. The water they drank was pure. They were at peace with God, at peace with each other, and at peace with creation. All was good.

In this perfect world, God placed two important trees - the tree of life and the tree of knowledge of good and evil. The fruit of the tree of knowledge of good and evil was the only fruit that was off limits. God provided Adam and Eve with plenty to eat from the other trees. They didn't need the forbidden fruit. God warned them, "You may freely eat the fruit of every tree in the garden — except the tree of the knowledge of good and evil. If you eat its fruit, you are sure to die" (Genesis 2:6-7 NLT).

They had one rule to obey. Eat freely, as much as you want from all the other trees, but don't eat from this ONE tree. If they disobeyed, there would be severe consequences. The warning was clear – eat of this tree's fruit and you will die. The responsibility of keeping the world peaceful was in their hands. As long as they followed God's direction, and didn't eat the fruit of this one tree, all would stay under control.

They were not robots. They had within their reach the opportunity and the freedom to rebel if they wanted. They were people made of flesh and blood. They were created with a will of their own. There wasn't an electric fence or a moat filled with hungry crocodiles that guarded the tree. They were able to freely walk up to it, take the fruit, and eat it. They had the freedom to ignore God's warning and disobey God's command IF they chose to do so. They had the capacity for sin.

God created each of us with the freedom to choose. We have the freedom to make our own decisions. We have the freedom to choose to obey God or disobey God. He created us this way because he loves us. Love always gives the other person a choice. Love cannot be forced or coerced. If you love someone, you set them free. That is true in all human relationships. That is exactly how God created Adam and Eve, and that is how he created each of us. He gave us free will to do as we choose.

Trouble in Paradise

Adam and Eve, however, had something none of us have ever had – a perfect world. While it was perfect, the potential for calamity was within their reach. The fallen angel Satan looked upon their situation and seized the opportunity to wreak havoc.

He set his sights on the people God had created in his own image. Since he couldn't gain control of heaven, he sought control of the earth and the people whom God had entrusted to rule it. He moved in to unleash the chaos on earth that he had started in heaven. He came to steal, kill, and destroy.

He didn't come with brute force. He came quietly. He was subtle in his approach. He was cunning and deceptive. That is the way he works. The Scriptures tell us that he is a master of deception. "Satan disguises himself as an angel of light" (2 Corinthians 11:14 NLT). On the surface his intentions may seem good, but at his core he is a devil through and through.

His strategy was simple but clever. He would use deception, lies, and temptation to influence Adam and Eve to sin. He began by asking them a question to plant a seed of doubt in their minds and hearts. He asked, "Did God really say you must not eat the fruit from any of the trees in the garden?" (Genesis 3:1 NLT).

He didn't force or insist that they go and eat from the tree of knowledge of good and evil. He didn't grab them and shove the fruit into their mouths. He simply planted a thought that would cause them to question God's goodness. It was inception. He knew that the decision to sin had to be their own and that it had to start with a thought. That is because Satan can't force us to do anything against our will. He can influence us, but he can't make decisions for us or control us.

Eve rejected Satan's temptation. "Of course we may eat fruit from the trees in the garden, it's only the fruit from the tree in the middle of the garden that we are not allowed to eat. God said, 'You must not eat it or even touch it; if you do, you will die'" (Genesis 3:2-3 NLT).

Rejected at first, Satan didn't give up. He had planted his seed of doubt in her heart and mind. He knew it would just take time to grow.

He came back later to water the seed. He lied to her. He told her, "You won't die!" (Genesis 3:4 NLT). Lies kill. Lies have the power to wreak havoc in our lives. Lies blind us to the truth. When we believe lies we become entrapped.

By lying to Eve, Satan hoped to convince her that what he said was more trustworthy than what God had told her. He wanted her to imagine how things could be if she would only trust him instead of God. He proceeded to tell her, "God knows that your eyes will be opened as soon as you eat it, and you will be like God, knowing both good and evil" (Genesis 3:5 NLT).

Satan wanted Adam and Eve to question God, his promises, and his goodness. He wanted to deceive them into believing that God was really holding out on them. Deception often contains 99% truth and 1% lie. That is its power. The 99% of truth easily hides the 1% of falsehood.

It was true that if they ate of the tree their eyes would be opened. They would know both good and evil. But not in a good way. They would come to know it by painful experience. Their eyes would be opened to heartache, problems, suffering, and death. He was trying to convince them that if they listened and took his advice, then their eyes would be opened to the real truth. But in reality he was blinding them to the truth.

Lies and deceit are powerful weapons. They cause us to believe in a reality that doesn't exist. The illusion often offers something better than what we currently have. The grass is greener on the other side. Lies appeal to our desires and emotions. When we exchange the truth for a lie, allowing ourselves to be deceived, it is difficult to break free. Once deceit grips us, it holds on tight with white-fisted knuckles. It blindfolds us and take us places we never wanted to go.

Satan wanted Eve to believe that what he was offering on the other side of temptation was better than what God had provided. He planted a seed of discontentment. He does the same with each of us.

He wants you to believe that the pleasure derived from what he is offering is better than anything God will provide. He wants you to be discontent with the good things God has provided for you. He wants you to forget about the consequences.

That seed of discontentment quickly took root and poisoned the fertile ground of contentment in Eve's heart. Satan planted, watered, and fertilized that seed. As it grew, it choked out her judgment. She lost sight of the consequences, forgetting what God had clearly told them would happen if they disobeyed.

She was blinded to Satan's intentions. Satan didn't come to enlighten them and offer them a better life as he promised; he came to steal, kill, and destroy everything good in Adam and Eve's life and in our world.

To be fair to Adam and Eve, we can all understand the experience of temptation that they faced. The Scriptures tell us that, "The temptations in your life are no different from what others experience" (1 Corinthians 10:13a NLT).

You may not have two trees in front of you to choose from, but you do have other tempting choices. Be honest on your taxes or cut corners. Tell the truth or lie to protect yourself. Flirt with the co-worker or head home to your spouse. Look at that webpage or shut down your computer. We can relate to Adam and Eve and understand the struggle they must have experienced.

Temptation is a universal phenomenon. We all understand it because we have all faced it. People in every age and every nation have experienced it. No one is immune. We have all given in to it at some point. "For everyone has sinned; we all fall short of God's glorious standard." (Romans 3:23 NLT)

While temptation is universal, God promises not to allow us to be tempted beyond what we can handle. He always provides a way of escape. Whenever you face temptation, God marks the way out with a bright red "Exit" sign to lead you out of the burning building. "And God is faithful. He will not allow the temptation to be more than you can stand. When you are tempted, he will show you a way out so that you can endure" (1 Corinthians 10:13b NLT). We only need to look for the exit and run towards the door.

God never tempts us. The Bible is clear about this. "And remember, when you are being tempted, do not say, "God is tempting me." God is never tempted to do wrong, and he never tempts anyone else" (James 1:13 NLT). While he *allowed* Adam and Eve to be tempted, he was not the one doing it.

Satan is the one who tempts. He plays to our selfish desires. "Temptation comes from our own desires, which entice us and drag us away. These desires give birth to sinful actions. And when sin is allowed to grow, it gives birth to death" (James 1:14-15 NLT). That is what happened to Adam and Eve. Satan tempted them, but ultimately they were being enticed by their own desires. They were living in Paradise, but they were on the verge of throwing it all away if they gave in.

Chapter 3

REBELLION
ON EARTH

It was in this moment of temptation that we find the reason why things were thrown out of control in our world. The most tragic event in all of human history occurred. "She saw that the tree was beautiful and its fruit looked delicious, and she wanted the wisdom it would give her. So she took some of the fruit and ate it. Then she gave some to her husband, who was with her, and he ate it, too" (Genesis 3:6b NLT).

Adam and Eve ate the forbidden fruit. With that one act of disobedience, they threw our world out of control. The black clouds of death, pain, and suffering rolled into Eden.

It might have tasted good initially, but it quickly soured their stomachs. That is how sin works. It looks good in the beginning but bites in the end. The forbidden fruit bit back. We don't know if they ate all the fruit or if they took a bite and threw the rest away in disgust. It really didn't matter at that point; it only took one bite. With one bite, they had crossed the line.

Sin has far reaching consequences. More than we first realize. The spouse who cheats. The father or mother who leaves the family. The lie spoken to cover the truth. Any time we take a bite of a forbidden fruit there are ripple effects. Your actions affect the lives of others around you. That initial choice to sin by Adam and Eve continues to impact us today.

Satan struck a deadly blow against humanity in the Garden of Eden that day. He took control of this world that God had originally entrusted to Adam and Eve. Satan became its god (2 Corinthians 4:4). He could now roam freely and bring chaos and destruction to it.

For Adam and Eve, the partial truth of Satan's lie was realized as their "eyes were opened" (Genesis 3:7 NLT). Their eyes were not opened in the way Satan had led them to believe; they were opened to guilt and shame. Feeling shame for the first time, they immediately sewed fig leaves to cover themselves. They felt the weight of their wrongdoing.

Could God have stopped them from eating of the tree? Yes. But in his love for them he allowed them the freedom to choose. With that freedom came responsibility for their decisions and actions. Adam and Eve were each responsible for their own sin, just as we are responsible for ours.

Their sin would be much more devastating than they realized. It would change everything. They suffered a spiritual death that day, a death that affected their souls, physical bodies, hearts, and minds. It separated Adam and Eve from their Creator. There was now a wall between them and God.

There are a lot of problems in our world, but the root of all the problems we experience is sin. It is the greatest catastrophe, epidemic, and tragedy our world has ever known. With Adam and Eve's disobedience, the creation and all that was once good was now contaminated.

Where there was once peace, now there was confusion. Where there was once order, now there was disorder. Where there was once eternal life, now there was death. Understanding the brokenness of your own life and our world begins here.

God's Response When We Sin

God is a loving Father, even in the face of rebellion. As a loving Father, he came to the garden just as he had in the past. He came seeking to spend time with his children. He came in love.

God must have felt the way any parent who has to discipline a child for misbehavior does. He was grieved over what they had done. He wanted the best for his children, but they had chosen not to follow his direction and to go their own way. That is the story of every one of us. "All of us, like sheep, have strayed away. We have left God's paths to follow our own" (Isaiah 53:6 NLT).

As God came walking in the garden in the cool of the day, Adam and Eve did something they had never done before; they hid among the trees (Genesis 3:8 NLT). Sin made them want to hide. It brought fear and insecurity. It sapped their confidence.

Just like Adam and Eve, we hide. We don't hide ourselves among the trees. Rather we hide ourselves behind false pretenses. We hide by covering up our secrets and shortcomings. We hide by not taking responsibility for our actions. We hide by shifting the blame to others. We have lost the confidence and assurance of living in a right relationship with God and others that existed in the beginning.

While sin might have deceived Adam and Eve into thinking they could actually hide from God, hiding was impossible. God saw everything. God knew everything. The Scriptures say, "Nothing in all creation is hidden from God. Everything is naked and exposed before his eyes, and he is the one to whom we are accountable" (Hebrews 4:13 NLT).

So God called out to Adam, "Where are you?" (Genesis 3:9 NLT). This wasn't a game of hide and seek. God knew their hiding place. God called out to Adam in mercy. Instead of ignoring Adam and Eve, God took the initiative to seek them out. Even though they turned their backs on him, God reached out to them. God longed to have friendship with the people he created, even though they had sinned against him.

He does the same with you. When you sin, he seeks you out. He calls to you. Even when you turn your back on him and hide from him, he doesn't give up on you. He loves you. He doesn't hurl a lightning bolt to strike you down; he comes with arms wide open to bring you back to him. He calls to your heart and asks, "Where are you?" He wants your relationship to be restored with him.

God "found" Adam in the Garden and asked him, "Who told you that you were naked?" and "Have you eaten from the tree whose fruit I commanded you not to eat?" (Genesis 3:11 NLT).

God knew the answer. This was a rhetorical question. He was giving Adam the opportunity to confess what had happened, to accept responsibility for his actions. Instead of accepting responsibility, Adam cast blame. He said, "It was the woman you gave me who gave me the fruit, and I ate it" (Genesis 3:12 NLT).

Adam blamed Eve. The honeymoon was over quickly as he threw Eve under the bus. He claimed it was her fault that he had sinned. As much as Adam wanted to cast the blame on someone else, he was guilty for his own actions.

The blame game still happens today. We deny any wrongdoing. It was someone else's fault. We deflect in order to avoid our own shortcomings and failings. It's easier to blame someone else than accept responsibility.

Eve blamed the serpent. "The serpent deceived me, and I ate" (Genesis 3:13 NLT). She claimed to be an innocent victim, too. Neither Adam nor Eve owned up to the sin. They were equally blameworthy.

God didn't blame but issued right judgment. We can always trust God to judge us fairly. He began with Satan. "I will cause hostility between you and the woman, and between your offspring and her offspring. He will strike your head, and you will strike his heel" (Genesis 3:15 NLT) .

This was both a punishment and a prophetic indication of God's plan. There would be hostility between people and Satan, an ongoing battle through the ages. But a descendant of Eve would ultimately defeat the work done by Satan in the Garden. Yes, Satan would bruise his heel and bring momentary pain and suffering to him, but ultimately he would crush Satan and win the final victory. The hope and promise God gave was that a future son of Eve would defeat the death, pain, and suffering unleashed in the garden and repair what Adam and Eve had broken.

In the mystery of God's plan, he would turn things around for our good. Even though a woman in the past first believed the lie and sinned against God, a woman in the future would believe the truth, obey God, and play an important role in redeeming what was lost.

Satan may have won the current battle, but God would win the final one. None of the actions of Satan, Adam, or Eve took God by surprise. The story was far from over. Satan may have manipulated

Adam and Eve, but God, in his wonder and wisdom, would turn Satan's manipulation back on him and bring good out of something bad.

The Curse

God came to Eve. "Then he said to the woman, "I will sharpen the pain of your pregnancy, and in pain you will give birth. And you will desire to control your husband, but he will rule over you" (Genesis 3:16 NLT).

Pain would become a normal part of giving birth for women. Getting pregnant and giving birth wouldn't be easy. And to make matters worse, there would be an ongoing struggle for power in the marriage relationship. Before the fall there was no such struggle. Husband and wife worked together in perfect harmony and unity. Not anymore. Eve's sin damaged that complementary relationship.

It was Adam's responsibility to protect Eve and the Garden. His punishment reflected that. "Since you listened to your wife and ate from the tree whose fruit I commanded you not to eat, the ground is cursed because of you. All your life you will struggle to scratch a living from it. It will grow thorns and thistles for you, though you will eat of its grains. By the sweat of your brow will you have food to eat until you return to the ground from which you were made. For you were made from dust, and to dust you will return" (Genesis 3:17-19 NLT).

In the Garden, life had come easily. That changed with Adam and Eve's sin. Life would not readily cooperate with men any longer. It would be a struggle, producing thorns and thistles. Thorns and thistles meant the ease and abundance Adam and Eve had experienced in the Garden was gone. Life would be hard. People would have to struggle to make a living. They would sweat and feel the ache in their bodies. They would experience frustration and difficulty in whatever work they did.

I experienced the frustration of the curse today. I stepped away from writing and thought I would pressure wash our driveway. I thought it would be a good break. It wouldn't take long, I thought. I was wrong. The motor kept cutting off. I would work for about five minutes, then spend the next 15 trying to get the motor running again.

And it was hot. I wiped the sweat from my brow as the temperatures soared above 90. I was hot, sore, and frustrated. Then to make things worse, the hose broke on the pressure washer and water went spewing everywhere. I was left with an unfinished project and new damages.

This wouldn't have happened in the Garden. Frustrating experiences like this are all part of the curse. The curse means things won't be easy and will often cause frustration. Work won't be easy. Relationships won't be easy. Raising children won't be easy.

So why didn't God keep us from having to go through this? Instead of cursing the earth, why couldn't he instead have responded to Adam after he sinned, saying, "No big deal Adam. You know, we all make mistakes. Just don't let it happen again."

Because that would be unfair and unjust and God is just. For there to be true justice in the universe, the guilty can't go free. In a just world, there must be punishment for wrongdoing. Even in human courts we expect justice to be carried out, so how much more should we expect a just God to carry out justice in his courtroom? And unlike human justice, God's acts of justice are always right. He is THE perfect judge. As a loving, holy, and just judge over his creation, God pronounced right judgments for the wrongdoing committed by Satan, Adam, and Eve.

The bodies of Adam and Eve would return to the dust from which they were created. While Adam lived a long life totaling 930 years, he eventually died just as God said he would. Eve died too. They died because they believed the lie and ate the forbidden fruit. As a result, they no longer had access to the tree of life that gave them the ability to live forever.

The Scriptures make it clear that sin and death came into the world through Adam in the beginning. "When Adam sinned, sin entered the world. Adam's sin brought death, so death spread to everyone, for everyone sinned" (Romans 5:12 NLT).

Our bodies are now subjected to pain, injury, sickness, disease, and ultimately death. We exchanged eternal life with immortal bodies for mortal bodies and a finite existence. There would be funerals, burials, and grief in this new world.

Death has spread throughout the entire human race. It is the most catastrophic result of Adam and Eve's sin. I am thankful for those who work to prolong life through medicine, science, nutrition, and fitness, but while those things help, they are only band aids applied to a fatal wound. They don't fix the problem.

God then banished them from the Garden.

"Then the Lord God said, 'Look, the human beings have become like us, knowing both good and evil. What if they reach out, take fruit from the tree of life, and eat it? Then they will live forever!' So the Lord God banished them from the Garden of Eden, and he sent Adam out to cultivate the ground from which he had been made. After sending them out, the Lord God stationed mighty cherubim to the east of the Garden of Eden. And he placed a flaming sword that flashed back and forth to guard the way to the tree of life" (Genesis 3:22-24 NLT).

Adam and Eve were no longer able to experience the safety and order found in the Garden. We can't either. All of us are outside the Garden. We long for it but can't have it.

The reason we feel discontent, as if we are missing out on life, is because *we are* missing out. We were created for the Garden, and that longing is still within us. We long to be there. We long to reenter it.

S.D. Smith writes:

> There are echoes of Eden in our pain, a longing to slide past the angel's burning sword, and though singed, reenter Paradise. The Bible and all human experience is haunted with our loss. Shortly after the Fall in Genesis 3 we read a refrain that's as hateful as it is perpetual. "And he died...and he died...and he died..." Death has us and we have death. We are handcuffed together in a prison we built while free.
>
> We feel the loss of innocence in our transition to adulthood, a taste of the death we live through. I believe we don't so much lose innocence, but we lose the illusion of innocence, and that all our long life is a waking up to who we are after the Fall. We are broken, and coming to understand this is a weight unlike anything we may otherwise bear, for it is the root of all our burdens. We wake up in ruins, lost in the woods of despair, searching for the slightest sign of the trail of hope.[4]

Maybe that is where you are.

You are waking up to who you are after the Fall. As you awaken, you may wonder if God is aware of all the bad that is happening in our world. You may question why he doesn't do something about it.

The truth is, God has been doing something about it and God is continuing to do something about it. God didn't create the world, then watch things unravel from a distance. He isn't aloof. He has been engaged in our world in ways we don't always see or understand. He is working out a bigger story -- his perfect plan of redemption.

While things may seem out of control to us, they are actually under the control of a sovereign God who is working out his sovereign plan. This sovereign plan has existed before the creation of the world and hasn't changed. While many of God's ways remain a mystery to us, he has revealed himself to us in a very powerful way. Thankfully, the story of the Fall in the Garden of Eden is not the end of our story.

We are so far removed from those events and that time that we may not realize that we, like Adam and Eve, have also rebelled. Knowingly or unknowingly, we are active accomplices in the rebellion that began with Adam and Eve. We are in rebellion against God's control, management, and sovereignty over our lives and world.

There might be something in you that feels it just isn't fair. You weren't there. You are not to blame. You couldn't control what they did. But the reality is that fairness was lost at that moment. We don't have control over what happened back then. Adam and Eve were our representatives in the beginning. And, truth be told, if we were there, we probably would have done the same thing.

The good news is that there is hope.

Part 2
JESUS DEMONSTRATED CONTROL

Chapter 4

GOD WITH US

There is hope because God doesn't abandon us after the Fall. He pursues us. He longs to bring us back. He doesn't just want us to know about him; he wants us to know him.

He promised a Messiah to break the curse, usher in his Kingdom, and take back control of this world. The Messiah would demonstrate control over all that is broken in our world: nature, people, angels, demons, sickness, and death.

People of faith waited for him. The earth longed for him. Prophets prophesied about him. The promise given long ago would come to pass. "For a child is born to us, a son is given to us. The government will rest on his shoulders. And he will be called: Wonderful Counselor, Mighty God, Everlasting Father, Prince of Peace. His government and its peace will never end" (Isaiah 9:6-7 NLT).

He was the one who would restore control. He was the one God promised to Adam and Eve and many other prophets through the ages. He would provide a bridge between our world and the other world. He would right the wrongs, rule with justice, and breathe new life into us and this old world. His arrival would change everything.

God could have sent the promised Messiah from heaven on a cloud. He could have sent him to earth on a heavenly chariot. After all, God's Messiah deserved a royal entrance.

Instead, God sent him as a baby. The Messiah came the route of human experience. As a man, he would experience all the hardship this world brings. Heartache and pain. The sweat of his brow. Even death. He would experience everything that we do.

The time came for his arrival. God sent an angel, a high-ranking messenger from the other world, to a young Jewish virgin named Mary to announce his coming. She was the chosen descendant of Eve. She would give birth to the promised son who would crush the head of the serpent.

Mary was afraid as the angel approached her, so he sought to comfort her, saying, "Don't be afraid, Mary...for you have found favor with God! You will conceive and give birth to a son, and you will name him Jesus...his Kingdom will never end" (Luke 1:30-31, 33b NLT).

God's message was directed to her and to all of us. He wanted us to know that he had not forgotten our plight. He had not given up on his plan to restore all that was broken and break the curse. The kingdoms of this world would end, but the Kingdom he would usher in would never end.

The angel said his name would be Jesus and they would call him Immanuel. "Look! The virgin will conceive a child! She will give birth to a son, and they will call him Immanuel, which means 'God is with us'" (Matthew 1:23 NLT).

God would be with us in the person of Jesus. God would be a part of our world. He would walk like us, look like us, and talk like us.

Most importantly, he would identify with us and everything we go through. He would be God with us, for us, and among us.

Mary was confused as to how all this could be. It seemed implausible. She was engaged to a man named Joseph, but they had abstained from sexual intercourse during their engagement. She didn't understand how she could possibly be pregnant. It didn't make sense.

The angel explained how it would happen, "The Holy Spirit will come upon you, and the power of the Most High will overshadow you. So the baby to be born will be holy, and he will be called the Son of God" (Luke 1:35 NLT).

It happened by a miraculous work of God. God and man came together as one. People called him both the Son of God and the Son of Man. He was both *divine* and *human*, the God Man.

He was *divine* because he was conceived by the work of the Holy Spirit. He had no human father. He didn't inherit original sin from Adam. In other words, the moral corruption and sinful nature of mankind wasn't passed down to him. He was holy, just as the angel had proclaimed.

At the same time, he was *human*. This was demonstrated by the fact that he was conceived in the womb of a woman. He had flesh and blood, just as we do. By taking on human flesh he would experience all the limitations that we experience. Pain. Weariness. Hunger. He would experience the variety of emotions we feel. He would experience the hardship and suffering that we do in a world under the control of Satan.

Jesus was both human and divine. That is the mystery of the divine incarnation that happened in the young virgin's womb. There have been many religious leaders throughout history, but none have entered the world as miraculously as this baby did.

Mary could have turned away in disbelief, discounting the divine plan announced by her angelic visitor. She could have asked him to pick someone else. She could have run away. But she didn't. She responded in faith. She chose to trust God's word and his plan. She didn't completely understand how all this could happen, but she chose to trust that God could accomplish the miraculous through her even if it didn't make sense. She chose to believe what the angel told her.

She said, "I am the Lord's servant. May everything you have said about me come true." And then the angel left her" (Luke 1:38 NLT).

Mary believed. She then had the difficult responsibility of explaining the situation to her fiancé. It is one thing to believe something God has revealed to you, but it is another thing to try and explain it to someone else. Our personal stories of encounters with God, especially those like Mary's that seem far-fetched, may often be met with skepticism and disbelief. We don't know how the conversation went between Mary and Joseph, but one thing was clear: Joseph didn't buy it.

"Joseph, her fiancé, was a good man and did not want to disgrace her publicly, so he decided to break the engagement quietly" (Matthew 1:19 NLT).

Joseph was a good man. It's hard to blame him for his disbelief. Mary's was an unbelievable story. But, out of love for her, he chose to treat her with dignity and respect. He could have had her stoned for committing adultery according to Jewish law[2] (Leviticus 20:10),

---

[2] (In Jewish custom, a man and woman engaged to be married were considered already married, although the consummation of the marriage was not to happen until after the wedding.)

but he didn't. While he must have felt hurt and betrayed, he still loved Mary and resolved to handle the matter quietly.

Joseph needed his own personal encounter with God to validate Mary's story. God knew that. He didn't leave Mary alone in her faith journey. He sent an angel to corroborate her story. Before Joseph was able to break the engagement, the angel Gabriel came to him in a dream to reassure him that what Mary had said was indeed true.

Matthew writes, "an angel of the Lord appeared to him in a dream. 'Joseph, son of David,' the angel said, 'do not be afraid to take Mary as your wife. For the child within her was conceived by the Holy Spirit'" (Matthew 1:20 NLT).

Like Mary, Joseph responded in faith to what God revealed to him.

"When Joseph woke up, he did as the angel of the Lord commanded and took Mary as his wife" (Matthew 1:24 NLT).

He believed and obeyed. That is what it takes to experience the power of God. That is how you come to know and experience God working through you. You take steps of faith by doing what you know you need to do next. It's that simple. You take the next step. Joseph did just that, stepping out in faith and marrying Mary.

The Birth of the King

Nine months later, Jesus was born in Bethlehem, just as the angels foretold. He was born in weakness and in humble circumstances. That is how the power of God is displayed.

"She gave birth to her first child, a son. She wrapped him snugly in strips of cloth and laid him in a manger, because there was no lodging available for them" (Luke 2:7 NLT).

None of the circumstances surrounding the birth of Jesus were what you would expect. He was born in a lowly stable, not a royal palace. He was born into poverty, not into riches. He was born to an average family, not an upper class one. God's son was placed in a feeding trough for animals, not the clean sterile environment you would expect for a king.

These circumstances reveal God's character to us. God is the Most High, but he is also gentle and humble in heart. He values humility and gives grace to the humble while opposing the proud because he himself is humble.

When you are humble, God supernaturally empowers you with his grace. His grace gives you strength. It doesn't numb you to the bad circumstances you might face, but it does give you the strength to face them.

Godly power doesn't come by way of might, money, or position. It comes through humility. By serving others. By putting others first. That is how the Messiah came. He gave up his divine privileges in heaven and took on the position of a servant on earth.

"Though he was God, he did not think of equality with God as something to cling to. Instead, he gave up his divine privileges; he took the humble position of a slave and was born as a human being" (Philippians 2:6-7 NLT).

While Jesus arrived in humble circumstances, the angels couldn't keep quiet about it. His birth was too remarkable an event. They heralded the good news of what had happened, but they didn't go about it the way the world would expect. Instead of telling the most prominent and influential people, the angels choose to announce Jesus' birth to unsuspecting shepherds.

Shepherds were the social outcasts of their day. They were despised in everyday life, considered second-class and untrustworthy. Shepherding was not a socially acceptable occupation. Yet these were the only other people to whom the angels announced the birth of the Messiah. That is how God works in our world.

The Scriptures teach us that, "God chose things the world considers foolish in order to shame those who think they are wise. And he chose things that are powerless to shame those who are powerful" (1 Corinthians 1:27 NLT).

God chooses the powerless to shame the powerful. He doesn't always choose the most talented, the most influential, the best looking, or the most socially accepted to accomplish his work. He doesn't need to. Rather, he often chooses those with little power, little influence, and low social standing to shame those who have great power, great influence, and high social standing. He opposes the proud and gives grace to the humble.

God sent an angel to tell the humble shepherds the news.

"Suddenly, an angel of the Lord appeared among them, and the radiance of the Lord's glory surrounded them. They were terrified" (Luke 2:9 NLT).

They responded as Mary did in the presence of the angel Gabriel. They were filled with fear. At the sight of such a glorious being and bright light, they might have expected a swift act of justice from God in punishment for their sins. But that wasn't why God sent this angel to them. The angel didn't come to punish but to bless. He came to bring the good news of the birth of the Messiah. The Messiah was sent to save the world, not condemn it.

The eternal, all-powerful, all-knowing God took on human flesh. He would be raised in a small town called Nazareth. God's choice for his Son's hometown showed once again how his power is displayed in weakness. Jesus' hometown was despised, he would be despised, and his plans of redemption would be despised by many.

There was nothing godlike in his appearance that caused people to take notice of him. "There was nothing beautiful or majestic about his appearance, nothing to attract us to him. He was despised and rejected— a man of sorrows, acquainted with deepest grief. We turned our backs on him and looked the other way" (Isaiah 53:2-3 NLT).

Jesus identified with anyone and everyone who has ever felt like an outcast. He understood what it was like to grow up in obscurity in ordinary circumstances. He understood what it was like to have people look at you and turn the other way. He wouldn't have been voted the most attractive or most popular. He looked like an ordinary boy of his day.

He also grew up as other boys did. He experienced human development. He grew taller. His voice changed. His body changed. He grew in wisdom. As a preteen, he sat in the temple, listened to the religious leaders, and asked them questions, maybe with a voice that squeaked as he went through puberty.

While Jesus was similar in appearance to other boys of his day, the religious leaders recognized that there was something different about him. They were amazed at his understanding and his answers. At this stage of his life, he enjoyed both the favor of God and the favor of all the people (Luke 2:52 NLT).

As Jesus grew up, he had to get a job. He decided to learn the trade of a carpenter. The God who created all things took a job in which he could create once again. He had originally created all things by speaking them into existence; now he would create things with his hands. He crafted the trees he had created into tables, chairs, and other furnishings. God rolled up his sleeves, went to work, and lived as one of us. And go to work he did. He began to take back control of the world, unveiling his plan to redeem all that had been lost in the Garden. He began his mission by first demonstrating control over temptation and the tempter who broke our world in the beginning.

Chapter 5

CONTROL OVER TEMPTATION

Where Adam Failed, Jesus Succeeded

Jesus began his ministry around 30 years of age. His first step was to succeed where Adam and Eve had failed. He had to resist the temptations of Satan.

He was led into the wilderness to be tempted by Satan. He wasn't led there by Satan, nor was he led there by curiosity. He was led there by the Holy Spirit. This was a divine assignment.

He fasted for 40 days in the wilderness in preparation for the battle. Then Satan came at Jesus' weakest moment to tempt him. Satan knows the best time to tempt us. He likes to tempt us when we are weak, tired, and hungry. He looks for the vulnerable moments.

Satan began similarly to the way he had tempted Adam and Eve in the Garden. He used food. Jesus was hungry, and Satan appealed to his humanity. He tempted Jesus to use his divine power to provide sustenance for himself.

"If you are the Son of God, tell these stones to become loaves of bread" (Matthew 4:3 NLT).

It would have been a simple thing for the one who created all the universe to turn a stone into a loaf of bread. Besides, Jesus needed something to eat; he was hungry. What would be wrong with performing a simple act to provide something he needed and deserved?

The problem was that Satan wanted Jesus to invoke his executive privilege. God chose to live as a man. He refused to use his supernatural power for his own benefit throughout his life, only using it for the benefit of others. Satan wanted him to bypass his humanity and invoke that executive privilege. Jesus resisted the temptation.

He said, "No! The Scriptures say, 'People do not live by bread alone, but by every word that comes from the mouth of God'" (Matthew 4:4 NLT).

He reminded Satan that man doesn't live by physical nourishment alone but by the spiritual nourishment God provides. We need the manna from heaven for our souls, just as our bodies need the bread of the earth. Spiritual nourishment is of paramount importance to our lives.

He also demonstrated that spiritual weapons are greater than physical weapons. Jesus used the spiritual weapon of his Father's word to fight back. Satan was a spiritual being, and he had to be fought with spiritual weapons. Jesus knew that, so he used the power of the Scriptures, our spiritual sword, to combat the tempter. The Scriptures have the power to penetrate the hearts of people, but they also neutralize the power of our spiritual foe, the devil. Jesus was teaching us this as he resisted.

Satan lost the first round, but he was persistent. He saw how Jesus used the Scriptures to defeat the first temptation, so he tried turning things around and using them against him. Knowing the power of the Scriptures, he twisted the meaning to test him.

"Then the devil took him to the holy city, Jerusalem, to the highest point of the Temple, and said, 'If you are the Son of God, jump off! For the Scriptures say, "He will order his angels to protect you. And they will hold you up with their hands so you won't even hurt your foot on a stone"'"(Matthew 4:5-6 NLT).

He was tempting him to once again bypass his humanity. Jesus corrected him.

"The Scriptures also say, 'You must not test the Lord your God'" (Matthew 4:7 NLT).

The power of the temptation was diffused. But Satan didn't give up. He tempted Jesus a third time.

"Next the devil took him to the peak of a very high mountain and showed him all the kingdoms of the world and their glory. "I will give it all to you," he said, "if you will kneel down and worship me" (Matthew 4:8-9 NLT).

That was what Satan was really after. That is what he has wanted since the beginning. He has always wanted God's place of power and control. He wants the worship, glory, and authority that only belong to God.

He used the same temptation to influence Adam and Eve to sin when he told them, "you will be like God" (Genesis 3:5 NLT). It was a temptation to be on equal footing with God, to be in total control.

For Jesus, it was a temptation to bypass the suffering that awaited him on the cross. Satan offered a shortcut, a way out of the physical pain and hardship that Jesus would have to experience as a man. He was saying to Jesus, "You don't have to experience all the pain and suffering that humanity goes through. There is an easy way out!" Thankfully for us, Jesus didn't take the easy way out. He resisted once again.

His resistance was critical in order to restore control to our world. Everyone else since Adam has failed this test. We have all given in to temptation, but where we were powerless, Jesus was powerful. He did what none of us have been able to do; he resisted. He demonstrated that he had control over all temptation. It had no power over him.

He then told Satan, "Get out of here, Satan...For the Scriptures say, 'You must worship the Lord your God and serve only him'"(Matthew 4:10 NLT).

Jesus chose the difficult road even though he knew it would involve suffering. He chose to identify himself with us. He didn't play the God card. He ended the battle and the confrontation with authority as he told Satan, "Get out of here!"

As our representative, he made it clear to Satan that the time of temptation and sin was coming to an end. His mission would ensure that. Jesus was the one who would banish temptation once and for all. In his coming Kingdom, there would be no more Satan and no more sin. He would bring things back under control.

Jesus fought and won the battle as a man on our behalf. Because he was a man, he was hungry and weak when Satan left. He must have been close to the point of collapse. Jesus needed physical sustenance. The angels came and provided for his needs.

From this point, Jesus began his three-year mission to usher in a Kingdom that would eventually overtake this world. He would prove that the Kingdom of Heaven is far greater than the kingdom of this world. He moved beyond his battle with Satan and began spreading the good news about his coming Kingdom.

Jesus made his way back to his boyhood hometown of Nazareth. One Saturday, on the Jewish Sabbath, he went to the synagogue as usual. As he stood up, the scroll of the Old Testament prophet Isaiah was handed to him. All eyes were focused on him as he read: "The Spirit of the Lord is upon me, for he has anointed me to bring Good News to the poor. He has sent me to proclaim that captives will be released, that the blind will see, that the oppressed will be set free, and that the time of the Lord's favor has come" (Luke 4:18-19 NLT).

After reading this passage, Jesus said something that shocked everyone who heard.

He said, "The Scripture you've just heard has been fulfilled this very day!" (Luke 4:21 NLT).

Jaws must have dropped. There were probably gasps of surprise and anger. How could a local carpenter's son who grew up in this small town be the long awaited Messiah? There was nothing special about his credentials or his appearance that would set him apart. They didn't believe he was the one. They didn't receive him or his message that day.

Jesus was disappointed, and he rebuked them for their unbelief. The people in the synagogue didn't take it well. They were furious, and their anger turned into violence. They became an angry mob, taking him to a cliff with the intent of throwing him over the edge to his death. Jesus however "passed right through the crowd and went on his way"(Luke 4:30 NLT).

He miraculously survived their attack. Why? It was not Jesus' time to die. That hour would come, but not now. Our Heavenly Father ensured his safe passage out of Nazareth until the time was right. The King was here and his Kingdom was coming. He set out from Nazareth to teach about his coming Kingdom and to demonstrate the power it had over this broken world. How and when this Kingdom would come would be difficult for many to understand. His message would be challenged, misunderstood, and refused by many, just as it had been in Nazareth.

Chapter 6

THE KINGDOM OF GOD RESTORES CONTROL

Jesus' teaching centered on his coming Kingdom, a Kingdom consisting of both the "already" and the "not yet". The "already" aspect of the Kingdom meant it was present in the here and now. The "not yet" aspect meant it would be consummated later in all its fullness. The Kingdom would eventually bring control to this out-of-control world, but it would happen gradually, over time. While we see and experience aspects of it now, we won't see the full effects until its consummation.

Even the disciples didn't understand this at first. They thought Jesus was going to set up his Kingdom immediately. It would be much later before they came to understand the truth. They, like us, must wait for the Kingdom's "not yet" aspect.

The religious leaders of the day challenged Jesus' teaching about the Kingdom by asking questions about when it would arrive.

They asked him, "When will the Kingdom of God come?"

Jesus replied, "The Kingdom of God can't be detected by visible signs. You won't be able to say, 'Here it is!' or 'It's over there!' For the Kingdom of God is already among you" (Luke 17:20-21 NLT).

Jesus was highlighting the "here and now" aspect of the Kingdom. It was already among them, for he was its king, the door, the gate, and the path by which all could enter. The Kingdom was wherever he was. The same is true today.

John Ortberg says, "The good news is especially that this world—the Kingdom of God—is closer than you think. It is available to ordinary men and women. It is available to people who have never thought of themselves as religious or spiritual. It is available to you. You can live in it—now."[5]

That is part of the mystery. The Kingdom, in a secretive way, has begun working its way through our world from the inside out. It begins by changing people internally, opening their hearts and spiritual eyes as the breath of heaven blows on them. This spiritual ushering in of the Kingdom precedes the Kingdom's physical coming in the end. Jesus explained this in parables.

"The Kingdom of Heaven is like a mustard seed planted in a field. It is the smallest of all seeds, but it becomes the largest of garden plants; it grows into a tree, and birds come and make nests in its branches" (Matthew 13:31-32 NLT).

It started small, but it will overtake all other kingdoms. Jesus intentionally chose a small, insignificant seed to make his point. The Kingdom of God, a seed planted in our world 2,000 years ago, began with a small group of followers, but it has grown into something much bigger. The number of people who claim to follow Jesus has quadrupled in the last 100 years alone. In 2014, there was 2.18 billion people claiming to follow Jesus and be part of His Kingdom.[6]

Jesus came to give the Kingdom to each of us freely. You have the opportunity to receive it, inherit it, and possess it, but you must seek it. You can't be passive about it. You have to pursue it. There are a lot of things you can seek out in this life. Physical needs. Relationships. Jobs. Dreams. Jesus said, "Seek the Kingdom of God above all else, and live righteously, and he will give you everything you need" (Matthew 6:33 NLT).

Seeking the Kingdom of God first requires you to rethink your pursuits. Instead of spending most of your time and energy taking care of yourself first, you must prioritize the things of God. In return, God promises to take care of your needs. This flies in the face of what our desires often tell us to do. Our tendency is to run after the things we need, but God says if we run after his Kingdom first, he will take care of everything else.

Part of seeking his Kingdom involves praying for its coming. Jesus said we should pray that his Kingdom would come and that his will would be done on earth as it is in heaven. When he taught his disciples to pray, he said they should pray about this first, even before they prayed for their daily needs. That is part of how we seek God's Kingdom first.

You must seek the kingdom because God will not force it upon you. You have the choice to reject it. While we can refuse it, we can't destroy it or its message. Many have tried through the ages, and many will continue to try. In fact, the opposition against the Kingdom will escalate to a final battle in the end. The Scriptures assure us, however, that opposition will fail.

The kingdom of this world will be overcome by the Kingdom of God in the end. In the last days, an angel will blast his trumpet and declare its arrival. "The world has now become the Kingdom of our Lord and of his Christ, and he will reign forever and ever" (Revelation 11:15 NLT).

Jesus wanted us to look forward to that day when his Kingdom will come in its full consummation, because in that day, the things that plague us now will no longer be out of control. Until then, he has given us a foretaste of what that time will be like. He set out to demonstrate how he and his Kingdom would restore peace to our natural world, a world that is longing to return to its original condition.

Chapter 7

CONTROL OVER NATURE AND FEAR

During his ministry, Jesus demonstrated his control over nature over and over again. He turned water into wine at a wedding party. He multiplied five loaves of bread and two fishes into enough food to feed over 5,000 people after a long day of ministry. He walked on water to catch up with his disciples. He spoke to a tree and made it wither by his word. The elements of our natural world were subject to his command. He was, is, and will always be the Creator and Sustainer of all creation.

Creation longs for his control, which will bring about its redemption. It longs to be redeemed by the one who has the power to do so. It longs to have the curse lifted. You can hear it in the wind, you can see it on the animal's faces, and you can feel it in your bones. Our world is crying out to shed itself of the old and broken and to be clothed with the new and restored eternal state promised by its Creator.

The current natural order of our world is beautiful, but it is also violent and unpredictable at times. It will continue to be that way until Jesus returns to restore it completely. Jesus said, "There will be famines and earthquakes in many parts of the world. But all this is only the first of the birth pains, with more to come" (Matthew 24:7-8 NLT).

Natural catastrophes will continue to inflict havoc on our world as it waits in pain to be reborn. In 2004, the Boxing Day Tsunami devastated the coast of Indonesia. It killed over 230,000 people. One third, or more than 76,000, of those killed were children. Jesus wanted us to know that tsunamis and other natural disasters will be a thing of the past once his Kingdom is ushered in.

Jesus Calms the Storm

Jesus and his disciples were crossing the Sea of Galilee on a small boat when a violent storm arose. It was bad enough that the disciples thought they would drown. They were scared.

What was Jesus doing while the storm raged? He was sleeping in the back of the boat. Unconcerned and at peace, he was tired, so he slept. The disciples, on the other hand, were afraid for their lives. They woke Jesus in desperation.

"When Jesus woke up, he rebuked the wind and said to the waves, "Silence! Be still!" Suddenly the wind stopped, and there was a great calm" (Mark 4:39 NLT).

"The disciples were absolutely terrified. 'Who is this man?' they asked each other. 'Even the wind and waves obey him!'" (Mark 4:41 NLT).

Jesus demonstrated that nature was under his control and that one day he would forever stop the storms that intrude on our lives. He wanted us to know that we don't have to be afraid when storms come our way.

"Then he asked them, "Why are you afraid? Do you still have no faith?" (Mark 4:40 NLT).

In order for us to experience the power of God, Jesus knew he had to confront the issue of fear in our lives. Fear will control you if you let it. It will keep you from experiencing God's power. Fear is a bully. If it goes unchallenged, it will continue to push you around, until you stand up to it in faith that is. Faith punches the bully of fear in the mouth and knocks it to the ground. Faith doesn't eliminate fear; rather, it gives you the power to move forward in the face of fear. It keeps fear from controlling you.

Not all fear is bad. We do experience healthy fear in life: The fear that reminds us to proceed cautiously. The fear that keeps us from driving too fast or recklessly. The fear that keeps us from taking unnecessary risks. That is not the kind of fear Jesus was talking about overcoming.

He was talking about overcoming the fear that keeps you from going where God wants to take you. The fear that keeps you from taking risks because you are unsure if he will provide. The fear that keeps you from moving forward because you are worried that you will fail. The fear that causes you not to trust him to see you through whatever situation you face. Faith overcomes this kind of fear.

If you don't deal with your fears, they will paralyze you. They will cause irrational thinking and actions, rob you of your faith, and lead you to doubt yourself and God. God may ask you the same thing he asked the disciples when they were facing the storm: "Why are you afraid?"

He wants you to know that he is there with you. He is in the boat with you in the midst of the storm. He wants you to know that there is no reason to be afraid when you trust in him.

God repeats to his people over and over throughout the Scriptures, "Don't be afraid". It's the recurring theme in what he told Joshua before he crossed into the promised land as Israel's new leader.

"This is my command—be strong and courageous! Do not be afraid or discouraged. For the Lord your God is with you wherever you go" (Joshua 1:9 NLT).

Like Joshua, we all have struggled with confidence at some point in our lives. For many of us, dealing with a lack of confidence can be a daily challenge. We need this reminder from our Heavenly Father.

John Eldredge said in his book *Wild at Heart* that every man struggles with this one question in his life: "Do I have what it takes?" I think men and women both struggle with this question.

We all wrestle with fear in some form or fashion. We wonder if we have what it takes to be a good spouse, a good parent, successful in our work, successful in life. At the root of the question, "Do I have what it takes?" is fear. We fear the answer is, "No, you don't". We have heard that from others, from ourselves, and from our enemy.

The Apostle Paul heard that in his life, too. He had gone without, endured hunger, and lacked financial stability. He was shipwrecked on several occasions. Yet he learned this truth through every situation he faced.

"For I can do everything through Christ, who gives me strength" (Philippians 4:13 NLT).

This doesn't mean that God will bless everything you do. It doesn't mean you will win the lottery or secure a big house, nice car, and carefree life by chanting this verse like a magical spell. It does, however, promise power to do what God calls you to do. Where God guides, he provides. He wants you to be strong and courageous as you move ahead in his plans for you. He wants to provide you with the power to overcome your fear through faith.

Jesus didn't stop there. He continued to show that he was in control over all things, including the demonic world that works long and hard to instill fear in all of us.

Chapter 8
CONTROL OVER SPIRITS

Demonic forces are constantly working to destroy the good things in your life and in our world. It is difficult to know all that they do and how much they have influenced you, your family, and the people around you. Probably much more than you realize. They work covertly behind the scenes. Their presence may be invisible to our eyes, but their work is seen in how they influence others and the world around us.

Jesus encountered and delivered people from their influence on many occasions. It one instance, two demon-possessed men came out to meet him. They possessed superhuman strength. Mark describes one of these men.

"This man lived in the burial caves and could no longer be restrained, even with a chain. Whenever he was put into chains and shackles—as he often was—he snapped the chains from his wrists and smashed the shackles. No one was strong enough to subdue him" (Mark 5:3-4 NLT).

These men were strong, and they were violent. The locals avoided this area. These guys were dangerous. It was like a scene from a horror movie. They wandered around the cemetery. They howled. They cut themselves with sharp stones (Mark 5:5 NLT). The demons were destroying these men's lives.

But Jesus was coming. He was coming to invade their territory and take back that which Satan had stolen from their lives. The men and the demons saw Jesus coming from a distance. They weren't happy. "They began screaming at him, "Why are you interfering with us, Son of God? Have you come here to torture us before God's appointed time?" (Matthew 8:29 NLT).

They knew they were being invaded and overpowered by someone much greater than them. They had no choice but to bow before the one who had all authority on heaven and earth. Mark writes, that one of the men "ran to meet him, and bowed low before him" (Mark 5:6 NLT).

The demons then took control of the men's voice again. They noticed a large herd of pigs feeding in the distance and begged Jesus, "If you cast us out, send us into that herd of pigs. 'All right, go!' Jesus commanded them. So the demons came out of the men and entered the pigs, and the whole herd plunged down the steep hillside into the lake and drowned in the water" (Matthew 8:31-32 NLT).

Just as demons have no regard for human life, they also have no regard for the lives of animals. As they entered the pigs, they caused them to kill themselves.

This also foreshadowed what Jesus would do to all members of the demonic world in the future. In the same way that the demon-filled pigs rushed into the lake, one day all demons will be cast into the eternal lake of fire. They will no longer be able to torment anyone. Instead, they will be tormented day and night forever.

These two men were restored back to their right minds. They were freed from their demonic oppressors. Jesus brought control into their lives, and that is what he wants to do for all of us. He wants to restore what Satan has stolen from you. He wants to deliver you from the evil one. Where Satan has inflicted harm and pain, Jesus wants to bring peace and healing.

Jesus shared his power with his disciples, sending them out to cast out demons. The demons obeyed and left the people the disciples ministered to. On one occasion, however, the disciples were unable to cast out an evil spirit from a boy.

The boy's father brought him to Jesus and asked him to help his son if he could.

"What do you mean, 'If I can'?" Jesus asked. "Anything is possible if a person believes." The father instantly cried out, "I do believe, but help me overcome my unbelief!" (Mark 9:23-24 NLT).

We, too, can believe and still have a hint of uncertainty buried in the corners of our minds. When we experience that uncertainty, we can do what this father did and pray with honesty, "I do believe, but help me overcome my unbelief."

Jesus answered his request. He commanded the spirit to come out of the child and never enter him again. Everyone there saw first-hand that Jesus was in control over the unseen spirits who torment us.

Jesus met with the disciples later about what had happened. They asked him why they hadn't been able to cast out the evil spirit the way they had others. Jesus told them that that kind of spirit could only be cast out by the power of prayer. They needed to sharpen their spiritual weapons, and so do we. We, too, have the power of praying in Jesus' name. Prayer is one of the greatest weapons we have to battle the spiritual authorities in our world.

And don't be naïve. The demonic world is not a fairy tale or a primitive belief of the past. That is what the demons would like for you to believe. There is a spiritual war going on all around you every day.

I first became aware of spiritual warfare when I was in my early twenties. I had a bad nightmare one night. I dreamt that there was a demon on my chest holding me down. He had his claws around my neck, choking the life out of me. I couldn't breathe. I awoke from the dream gasping for air.

As I did, I felt like there was still a presence pressing heavily on my upper body. The room was very cold. I was overcome with fear. I struggled to get words out. I began to pray out loud. After I prayed, I recited some verses from the Bible that lay close to my bed. Then the presence left the room.

I found out that I wasn't alone in my experience. The medical community calls this phenomenon sleep paralysis, and it's been happening to people all over the world for a long time.

This is the historical background according to WebMD: "Over the centuries, symptoms of sleep paralysis have been described in many ways and often attributed to an "evil" presence: unseen night demons in ancient times, the old hag in Shakespeare's Romeo and Juliet, and alien abductors. Almost every culture throughout history has had stories of shadowy evil creatures that terrify helpless humans at night. People have long sought explanations for this mysterious sleep-time paralysis and the accompanying feelings of terror."[7]

I don't think their description explains the temperature drop in my room that night. I have had many medical issues in my life, but I can assure you that this was a spiritual issue and had to be fought with spiritual weapons.

I know that we still face spiritual forces in the unseen world that are powerful enemies. The Apostle Paul wrote, "For we are not fighting against flesh-and-blood enemies, but against evil rulers and authorities of the unseen world, against mighty powers in this dark world, and against evil spirits in the heavenly places" (Ephesians 6:12 NLT).

The Apostle Paul tells us to pray as we battle the enemy. Prayer crosses over from our world into the other world. It allows us to battle evil beings we can't see.

In the book of Revelation, we see an angel taking the prayers of God's people and mixing them with incense on a gold altar before God's throne. He then hurls the mixture down to earth. It causes thunder, lighting, and an earthquake. Our prayers are powerful! (Revelation 8:4 NLT).

Jesus said when we pray we should ask, seek, and knock. Our prayers should be continual and perpetual. We should pray and not give up, asking the Father to deliver us from the evil one.

Prayer is your spiritual lifeline. It expresses your dependence on God. Max Lucado says prayer, "acknowledges our inability and God's ability."[8] When we pray, we invite God to get involved in our situation. We invoke the power of his name in the spiritual realm. We unleash heaven on hell. We can do all of this because Jesus has all authority on heaven and on earth. He has power over the demonic forces influencing our lives and the lives of those around us.

When God Says, "No!"

The Apostle Paul understood the importance of prayer. He was a prayer warrior. Whenever he faced a personal situation that brought him pain, he prayed about it. One of the things he prayed about was a thorn in his flesh.

We aren't sure exactly what Paul's thorn in the flesh was. All we know for sure is that it was harassing him. Paul wanted it gone, so he prayed. He pleaded with God not once, but three times, to take it away. He followed Jesus' teaching on prayer, asking, seeking, and knocking persistently.

God answered him each time, but not in the way Paul wanted.

"No", he said. "I'm not taking it away".

Sometimes God answers, "Yes". Sometimes he says, "No". And sometimes he says, "Wait". When he says, "No," or "Wait," we can continue to pray. That is what Paul did. He pleaded with God. "We do not simply spread our thought out before God, but we offer it to Him, turn it on Him, bring it to bear on Him, press it on Him."[9] We take prayer seriously.

We should wrestle with God in prayer much like Jacob did.

When Jacob thought his brother Esau was coming to attack him, he wrestled in prayer all night. His wrestling in prayer wasn't just a spiritual exercise; it was a physical one. God came in human form and wrestled with him until daybreak. Unable to win the match physically, God "touched Jacob's hip and wrenched it out of its socket" (Genesis 32:25 NLT).

Jacob still wouldn't let go. He pleaded for God to bless him. After the struggle was over, God granted his request and changed Jacob's name to Israel, a name that meant "he strives with God."[10] The nation of Israel and the Jewish people trace their lineage back to Jacob, the prayer wrestler. We, too, need to wrestle with God in prayer.

Paul prayed like Jacob. God told him no, and he asked a second time, and then a third. On the third request, God gave him an important truth and revelation. "My grace is all you need. My power works best in weakness" (2 Corinthians 12:9 NLT).

God may answer some of your prayers that way, too. It could be that he wants you to endure the pain through the power of his grace. He wants you to experience his power working through you while you are weak. He wants you to experience his grace carrying you. He wants you to understand that his grace is sufficient for you. He wants you to appreciate that his grace is perfected in weak vessels like you and me.

Paul accepted God's answer and made a resolution.

"I am glad to boast about my weaknesses, so that the power of Christ can work through me. That's why I take pleasure in my weaknesses, and in the insults, hardships, persecutions, and troubles that I suffer for Christ. For when I am weak, then I am strong" (2 Corinthians 12:9b-10 NLT).

Pain has a way of getting our attention, doesn't it? C. S. Lewis said, "We can ignore even pleasure. But pain insists upon being attended to. God whispers to us in our pleasures, speaks in our conscience, but shouts in our pains: it is his megaphone to rouse a deaf world."[11] Pain and weakness are the platforms through which God's power can be displayed in your life. Be like the Apostle Paul. Pray. Then pray again. Then pray some more. If he answers,

"No", then boast about your weakness so the power of God may rest on you, too.

While God didn't remove the thorn in Paul's flesh at that time, one day he will remove all the weaknesses and illnesses from our bodies. Jesus continued to show that he has power to heal all of our diseases.

Chapter 9

CONTROL OVER SICKNESS

During his time on earth, Jesus gave us a foretaste of what will take place when his Kingdom is fully established. On that day, he will fully remove the infirmities that plague our bodies.

Our bodies were originally created to live forever. After the Fall, the physical makeup of our bodies changed. We lost access to the tree of life. Since then, every person has experienced sickness in some form.

Sickness and disease are major elements of our out-of-control world world. We spend a lot of money trying to stay healthy. The United States alone spent $3 trillion on healthcare in 2014.[12] Thousands of people spend thousands of hours and thousands of dollars from day to day looking for cures, caring for the sick, and trying to prevent illness. Still, we have been unable to eradicate the world of disease and sickness.

Jesus wanted us to know that he will eradicate all sickness. He showed us that by healing people everywhere he went. We find many accounts of Jesus healing individuals and the masses.

Jesus told a paralyzed man to stand up, and he did. He touched the eyes of a blind man, and he could see. He put his finger in the ears of a man who was deaf and enabled him to hear. A woman with a bleeding disorder touched the fringe of his robe and was instantly healed. Jesus healed wherever he went. There was healing power flowing out from all around him as he walked through the crowds. Jesus was reversing the effects of the curse.

"This fulfilled the word of the Lord through the prophet Isaiah, who said, "He took our sicknesses and removed our diseases" (Matthew 8:17 NLT).

Some people misunderstand the application of this verse. They look back to Jesus' healing ministry and assume that all people will be healed this side of heaven if they have enough faith. They wrongly believe that if a sick person isn't healed, then he or she must have a faith issue. They point back to the promise in Isaiah, "with his wounds we are healed" (Isaiah 53:5 ESV).

It is important to understand the "not yet" aspect of the Kingdom when it comes to physical healing. Jesus does heal people in the here and now. From time to time, he grants us a foretaste of the physical healing that he will grant us fully in the future. It is my personal experience, however, that most don't receive their healing in the here and now.

A lady with an ongoing illness came to me one day in distress. Her illness had disabled her for a few years. Many people had been telling her that illness doesn't come from God and that he wanted her well. She just needed to have faith that God would heal her. She did have faith. But God answered her much like he did the Apostle Paul - "No, my power is made perfect in weakness."

I assured her that it wasn't due to a lack of faith as some had told her. I shared the story of Paul's thorn in the flesh and how God told him "No" when he asked for healing. She then asked me, "Did I do something wrong to deserve my illness? Am I being punished?" This was very similar to a question I'd heard asked at a retreat for families living through pediatric cancer.[3]

At the retreat, one of the pastors asked the participating parents if they ever felt responsible or guilty for their children's cancer. To my surprise, almost all of them said, "Yes." They wondered what they had done wrong to cause disease to afflict their children. When I heard their response, I was heartbroken. Not only were these parents dealing with the hardship of caring for their kids struggling with cancer, but they were also carrying a heavy load of guilt because they felt responsible for their children's condition.

You may have wondered the same thing if you or a family member has an illness, disease, or disability. You may question whether you or the afflicted person did something wrong to deserve the condition. You are not alone. The disciples wondered this, too.

They approached a man born blind and wanted to know, "Why was this man born blind? Was it because of his own sins or his parents' sins?" (John 9:1-2 NLT).

They assumed that the blind man's physical disability was caused by a sin either he or his parents had committed. Jesus took this opportunity to clear up the confusion.

"It was not because of his sins or his parents' sins,"…"This happened so the power of God could be seen in him" (John 9:3 NLT).

---

[3] The retreat was hosted by Blue Skies Ministries. Blue Skies Ministries helps bring the hope of Christ to families living through pediatric cancer. http://www.blueskiesministries.org/

71

His blindness was a platform through which to display the power of God. Jesus wanted us to know that sickness, illness, and physical handicaps aren't necessarily the result of specific sins you or your family committed in the past. There isn't always a direct correlation between physical ailments and sin.

Then Jesus "spit on the ground, made mud with the saliva, and spread the mud over the blind man's eyes. He told him, 'Go wash yourself in the pool of Siloam'... So the man went and washed and came back seeing" (John 9:6-7 NLT).

This blind man was enabled to see because the King and the Kingdom had invaded his world. Jesus wanted all of us to see what the power of God can do to our broken bodies. It will heal and restore them. Sometimes in the "here and now" and most definitely in the life to come.

While not all sicknesses can be traced back to specific sins, some can. Some illnesses and diseases, such as fetal alcohol syndrome or lung cancer caused by lifelong smoking, may be the result of specific sins. In instances like these, there are direct correlations between illness and the actions leading to it. But in the blind man's case, the affliction was not the result of his sin or his parent's sin, as the disciples suspected. It was the result of living in a fallen world.

Not every bad situation comes about because of something you or someone else has done. Sometimes bad things just happen. And when they happen, God can use them to display his glory.

You may have heard of Joni Eareckson Tada. At age 17, she was severely paralyzed in a diving accident that left her a quadriplegic, paralyzed from the shoulders down. She is in her sixties now and has also battled chronic pain and breast cancer. Joni has a lot of faith but has not been physically healed yet.

God has, however, healed another aspect of her life. She said, "I believe I have been healed — just not in the way that others expect." [13] She explained that her soul has been healed, which, she said, is more important than bodily healing. She has experienced a spiritual healing that has given her peace and joy in the midst of her suffering. She has experienced the "already" aspect of the Kingdom, even though she hasn't been physically healed, and she awaits the day when she will be physically and spiritually whole in the other world.

When that day comes, she wants to bring her wheelchair to heaven and put it in the corner as a reminder of how it made her more dependent on Jesus. She said she will tell Jesus, "the weaker I was in that thing, the harder I leaned on you." [14]

Anyone who has placed their faith in Jesus and has a disability, disease, or any other health issue, can look forward to being healed in the coming Kingdom. The healing ministry Jesus demonstrated while on earth gives us that hope. It showed us what he will do in heaven for all of us. There will be no more handicapped parking spaces, hospitals, or chemotherapy. 100% of the people in heaven will be completely healed!

While that is true, we will all succumb to death at some point in our lives. Death is a guarantee. That is a harsh reality, but the good news is that Jesus demonstrated control over death, too. Because of that, there is hope even in the face of death.

Chapter 10

CONTROL OVER DEATH

In my experience, the death of someone close to us is the hardest thing we can experience in this world. It is the worst consequence of Adam and Eve's disobedience.

Jesus experienced the pain of losing someone when his friend Lazarus died. Jesus arrived at the scene four days after Lazarus had been buried.

Martha, Lazarus' sister, had sent for Jesus days earlier with the hope that he would come and heal her brother. She expressed her confusion and disappointment to Jesus about his delay in coming.

She said, "Lord, if only you had been here, my brother would not have died" (John 11:21 NLT).

She had watched Jesus heal many others. She knew he had the power to heal the sick, and she couldn't understand why he hadn't come in time to help his friend and her brother.

If you have lost someone you love, you may have felt that way, too. You may have said, "God, if only you had..." If only you had been here. If only you would have prevented this. If only you would have warned me. If only.

The truth is, God often doesn't respond the way we expect or hope because he has something better in mind. In those moments, we can become disappointed or disillusioned if we lose sight of the bigger picture. In the case of Lazarus, there was good reason Jesus didn't respond the way Mary and Martha had hoped he would. God had much bigger plans.

Jesus said to Martha, "I am the resurrection and the life. Anyone who believes in me will live, even after dying. Everyone who lives in me and believes in me will never ever die. Do you believe this, Martha?" (John 11:25-26 NLT).

Jesus asked Martha a pointed question. Do you believe?

I think at some point in our lives, Jesus asks us all the same things. Do you believe I am who I say I am? Do you believe I have power over death? Do you believe I can give you eternal life?

Martha responded with faith and confidence. "Yes, Lord," she told him. "I have always believed you are the Messiah, the Son of God, the one who has come into the world from God" (John 11:23-27 NLT).

Martha believed. She believed Jesus had all power over death. She believed in the resurrection of the dead. She believed that Jesus was Lord and the Son of God. She believed without seeing. Soon her faith would be realized.

Belief always precedes the blessing. Belief always precedes the miracle. Belief always precedes the door being opened to life after death.

Martha went and told Mary, her sister, that Jesus had arrived. When Mary came to Jesus, she fell at his feet. With tears in her eyes, she echoed what Martha had said: "Lord, if only you had been here, my brother would not have died" (John 11:32 NLT).

They must have talked about this together in his absence. Neither of them could understand why he had delayed in coming. Lazarus wouldn't have died if Jesus would have been there.

Jesus was moved by the heartfelt loss of Mary, Martha, and all those gathered. "When Jesus saw her weeping and saw the other people wailing with her, a deep anger welled up within him, and he was deeply troubled" (John 11:33 NLT).

Jesus experienced what it was like to feel grief as a man. He experienced his humanity. As a man, he hurt. But as God, he had the power to do something about it. So he went to the tomb where Lazarus was buried. When he arrived, he was overcome with sorrow. His emotions overpowered him. He wept. It was not just a few tears that leaked slowly out of the corners of his eyes but a flood of tears that poured forth as he expressed his profound sorrow over what death had done to his friend.

If Jesus grieved, then it is normal for us to grieve as well. Some may assume that with faith, you don't need to grieve. Don't believe that. Jesus didn't. Grief is not a sign of weakness, nor is it a lack of faith. It is the price of love. When you love hard, you hurt hard.

When we grieve, Jesus grieves with us. When we hurt, he hurts. When we weep, he weeps. He empathizes with us in our deepest pain.

Jesus was angry, too. He was angry at what death and grief had done to our world. He was angry at the hurt and pain that accompanies death. He was angry that death had torn apart what God had created and joined together. He was angry at our greatest enemy since the Fall. Jesus' anger lets us know that we, too, can be angry when death takes those we love. It is a normal human emotion.

Jesus' anger moved him to action when he came to Lazarus' tomb. "Roll the stone aside," Jesus told them (John 11:38-39 NLT). As the people rolled the stone away, Martha protested to Jesus before he entered the tomb. "Lord, he has been dead for four days. The smell will be terrible" (John 11:39 NLT).

Jesus told Martha, "Didn't I tell you that you would see God's glory if you believe?"(John 11:40 NLT).

So they rolled the stone aside. Then Jesus looked up to heaven and said, "Father, thank you for hearing me. You always hear me, but I said it out loud for the sake of all these people standing here, so that they will believe you sent me." Then Jesus shouted, "Lazarus, come out!" (John 11:40-43 NLT).

When the Creator of life calls out to you, you will arise! The power of Jesus rose Lazarus from the dead. He walked out of that smelly tomb wearing the grave clothes he was buried in. "Jesus told them, 'Unwrap him and let him go'" (John 11:44 NLT).

There must have been gasps. Tears of joy. Shouts of excitement. That was all the proof that many needed that day to believe Jesus was the Lord. He proved that he was the resurrection and the life. He backed up who he said he was with action. He proved that he held the keys to life and death. He proved that if we believe in him, even though we die, we can live again.

This is the greatest message all of us need to hear. As thankful as I am for the progress of medicine, science, and technology, none of those disciplines will ever be able to bring us and our loved ones back from the dead. Only Jesus can do that. In his Kingdom, death will be a thing of the past.

The Death and Resurrection of Jesus

Later it would come time for Jesus to experience death himself. His death would be very different from all others, for he would carry the sins of the world. He was the only one who could remove the curse of sin. He was the only one who could make the full payment for our sins. That payment would require his death on a cross.

To bring about control again, he would have to give up control. He had to yield his will to his Heavenly Father's will. And the Bible shares the reality of the struggle Jesus faced the night before his crucifixion.

That night, he withdrew to a garden to pray. It was in a garden that the first battle was lost, and it would be in a garden that the last battle was won. Jesus was in agony as he wrestled with God in prayer. He prayed earnestly. The Bible says that his sweat became like great drops of blood falling down to the ground.

As Jesus was experiencing physical and emotional trauma, he prayed, "My Father! If it is possible, let this cup of suffering be taken away from me. Yet I want your will to be done, not mine" (Matthew 26:39 NLT).

Jesus asked his Father if there was any other way for our sins to be removed. Was there a way that didn't include a cross? There wasn't. This was the only way. Jesus was willing to do it for our sake and for the sake of his Father's will.

Jesus' prayer and attitude in that moment shows us all how we must live in a world gone out of control. If we are going to experience

God's power and his will for our lives, then we must surrender our will to our Heavenly Father's will. When faced with difficult situations in our lives, we should pray, "Your will be done." We have to trust that his plan is better than ours, even when the path is difficult. That is what Jesus did.

The path of suffering for Jesus began. The soldiers and officers of the Jews came to arrest him. As they sought to take Jesus, Peter drew his sword. He wasn't going down without a fight. He swung his sword and cut off the ear of the high priest's servant.

Jesus reprimanded Peter and explained that his Kingdom would not come by force, but by sacrifice. "So Jesus said to Peter, 'Put your sword back into its sheath. Shall I not drink from the cup of suffering the Father has given me?'" (John 18:11 NLT).

Jesus didn't the need the sword of Peter at this moment but the power that could only come from his Heavenly Father. If force was all that was required to win the battle, he had plenty at his disposal. "Don't you realize that I could ask my Father for thousands of angels to protect us, and he would send them instantly?" (Matthew 26:53 NLT). Force wouldn't win this war. Surrender would.

Jesus reached out and touched the man's ear and healed him, but even the miraculous healing didn't change the minds of those who'd come to arrest him. They bound him and led him away. This was all part of God's sovereign plan.

The Trials of Jesus

It would be a long sleepless night for Jesus. He endured three series of Jewish trials, and then he was handed off to Pilate, the Roman governor, to be sentenced.

The King of the other world was tried before the kings of this world. Pilate asked him if he was indeed a king. Jesus answered him. "My Kingdom is not an earthly kingdom. If it were, my followers would fight to keep me from being handed over to the Jewish leaders. But my Kingdom is not of this world" (John 18:36 NLT).

Pilate didn't get it. He didn't get the idea that there was a greater Kingdom than the Roman Empire. He couldn't see beyond his world. This still happens today. People get caught up in political parties and candidates. They believe the kingdoms of this world are greater than the Kingdom of Heaven. Pilate fell into that same trap.

Nonetheless, Pilate determined that Jesus was not guilty of a crime. So he sought the will of the people. Then he went out again to the people and told them, "He is not guilty of any crime. But you have a custom of asking me to release one prisoner each year at Passover. Would you like me to release this 'King of the Jews'?" (John 18:38-39 NLT).

The crowd, stirred up by the religious leaders, shouted back, "No! Not this man. We want Barabbas!" (Barabbas was a revolutionary) (Matthew 18:40 NLT).

Pilate complied. He released Barabbas. Barabbas, who was a rebel and a murderer, got to walk free. The guilty went free and the innocent paid the price. Barabbas deserved to be punished. Jesus didn't.

The truth is, Barabbas' story is our story, too. We can look at Barabbas and see ourselves. We are rebels. We are guilty. Yet we get to walk free because Jesus took our place.

Pilate then asked the crowd, "Then what should I do with this man you call the king of the Jews?" (Mark 15:12 NLT).

Asking the people for their opinion is not always the best option. And just because the majority of people think something is right, that doesn't make it right. The will of the people is often wrong. They shouted back, "Crucify him!" (Mark 15:13 NLT).

Then Pilate had Jesus flogged.

Jesus was flogged with a whip that was made out of strips of leather. At the end of the leather were pieces of bone and lead. The Jews limited the number of whippings to 40, but no such limitation was recognized by the Romans. Victims of Roman flogging often didn't survive. Jesus was badly beaten.

These wounds were necessary if we were going to be healed. Sin had to be punished, and Jesus took that punishment on himself. The prophecies had told us that this must take place. "But he was pierced for our rebellion, crushed for our sins. He was beaten so we could be whole. He was whipped so we could be healed" (Isaiah 53:5 NLT).

On top of the physical pain, all of hell mocked him. "The soldiers wove a crown of thorns and put it on his head, and they put a purple robe on him. 'Hail! King of the Jews!' they mocked, as they slapped him across the face" (John 19:1-3 NLT).

They mocked his control and his kingship. The other gospels tell us that they punched him in the face. They spit on him. They disrespected his role and his authority in every way possible.

The Bible doesn't tell us, but I wonder if Satan whispered in Jesus' ear, "If you would have bowed to me in the wilderness and worshipped me, you could have bypassed all of this." He could have hissed, "I told you there was an easier way." Jesus remained steadfast.

When the beatings stopped, he was brought back to Pilate.

Pilate wanted to have him released. He found no basis for crucifying Jesus. But the people and the Jewish leaders insisted that he be crucified. They claimed that he had violated their law by claiming to be the Son of God.

Pilate turned to Jesus again to ask him more questions. Jesus sat in silence. "Why don't you talk to me?" Pilate demanded. "Don't you realize that I have the power to release you or crucify you?" (John 19:10 NLT).

Jesus showed Pilate something important about his control over an out-of-control world. He told him, "You would have no power over me at all unless it were given to you from above" (John 19:11 NLT).

Whatever power Pilate had at that moment was not of his own merit. It had been given to him by God. Jesus wanted us to know that even in the face of the evil actions of others, God is in control. Nothing can happen outside of God's sovereign control.

Pilate then handed Jesus over to be crucified.

Jesus carried his own cross to the place of his execution. On the way, he was so weakened by the flogging that a man named Simon was pressed into service to carry the cross for him the remainder of the way.

On the hill of Golgotha, "the soldiers nailed him to the cross. They divided his clothes and threw dice to decide who would get each piece. It was nine o'clock in the morning when they crucified him" (Mark 15:24-25 NLT).

As people came by, they mocked him. They hurled insults at him. They shook their heads at him in disgust. All of this was done to mock his control. The sign, the purple robe, the staff, and the crown of thorns scorned the claim that he was king. It was an all-out assault on his control over all things. Even one of the criminals being crucified next to him joined in and ridiculed him.

Jesus endured overwhelming agony on the cross. He suffered greatly as his life ebbed away. Amazingly, he had the power to stop the suffering if he wanted. He had the power to come off the cross. Instead, he showed what may have been greater power by staying there.

He told his disciples prior to that day, "The Father loves me because I sacrifice my life so I may take it back again. No one can take my life from me. I sacrifice it voluntarily. For I have the authority to lay it down when I want to and also to take it up again. For this is what my Father has commanded" (John 10:17-18 NLT).

It wasn't nails that held him to the cross, but love. If you have ever wondered if God loves you, the cross settles that question once and for all.

In the midst of the mockery, pain, and suffering, Jesus said something incredible to the people who had murdered and defiled him. It defied all logic. Where it is our nature to want retribution when others wrong us, it is God's nature to forgive those who wrong him. Jesus said in his last moments, "Father, forgive them, for they do not know what they are doing" (Luke 23:34 NLT).

The people he had created in his own image rebelled against him. The soldiers crucified him. His disciples abandoned him. Yet he responded with forgiveness. No lightning bolts from heaven, only words of grace. He had allowed Adam and Eve to rebel in the Garden, and now the King was willingly giving his life to pay the price for our treason on the cross. He gave so we could have.

The Death of Jesus

Before Jesus died, he uttered the most victorious words in all of history, "It is finished!" (John 19:30 NLT).

The sacrifice was made. The curse was broken. The veil was torn. "At that moment the curtain in the sanctuary of the Temple was torn in two, from top to bottom" (Matthew 27:51 NLT).

We were no longer separated from God. The earth shook and the rocks split. The veil between our world and the other was torn in two. The dead came back to life. "The bodies of many godly men and women who had died were raised from the dead. They left the cemetery after Jesus' resurrection, went into the holy city of Jerusalem, and appeared to many people" (Matthew 27:52-53 NLT). This was not a zombie apocalypse. These were real people who came back to life from the grave.

After Jesus' death, his spirit entered heaven and sat down at the right hand of God. There were no more sacrifices to make. No more goats to kill. No more lambs to slaughter. The perfect lamb of heaven had been slain, and that was all that was needed from that point on. The sacrifice he had made for our sin was good for all eternity. Everything that needed to be done to bring things back under control was completed that day.

Jesus did what no one else could do. He cancelled our sin debt. Where we were powerless, Jesus was all-powerful. Where we didn't have the moral strength to conquer sin, Jesus did.

Meanwhile, the disciples were hiding. They were scared. They were unsure of what to do. Their King was dead, and their hopes were dashed.

The chief priests and Pharisees went to Pilate. They told him to give the order for Jesus' tomb to be made secure. They wanted to make sure that the disciples couldn't come and steal his body. There wasn't much to worry about, though; they were hiding. Pilate complied with the priests' request and placed a guard at the entrance to the tomb.

Neither the Roman guard, the Jewish leaders, nor Satan had the power to keep the body of Jesus in the tomb. He was in control over them and the grave. Death couldn't defeat him, and the grave couldn't hold him. As Tony Campolo said in a famous sermon, "It's Friday, but Sunday's coming."

The Resurrection of Jesus

Some women who were followers of Jesus went to the place where he was buried early Sunday morning. To their surprise, they found his tomb empty. "They found that the stone had been rolled away from the entrance. So they went in, but they didn't find the body of the Lord Jesus" (Luke 24:2-3 NLT).

Jesus was gone. They were puzzled. Had someone stolen his body?

All of a sudden, two angels appeared. The women were scared and bowed to the ground. The angels said, "Why are you looking among the dead for someone who is alive? He isn't here! He is risen from the dead! Remember what he told you back in Galilee, that the Son of Man must be betrayed into the hands of sinful men and be crucified, and that he would rise again on the third day" (Luke 24:5-6 NLT).

That was the greatest message ever heard! He is risen! That is why we can have hope! Death is not the end. There is life in the other world if we choose to receive it. That is the hope of the gospel.

Jesus came to visit his followers to prove to them that he had truly been resurrected. The disciples were hiding out together, trying to figure out what to do next, when Jesus made a surprise visit.

"Jesus himself was suddenly standing there among them. 'Peace be with you,' he said. But the whole group was startled and frightened, thinking they were seeing a ghost!" (Luke 24:36-37 NLT). He wanted them to know that he was not dead but alive.

Jesus wanted to assure them that he wasn't a ghost. He had flesh and bones, a resurrected body. He invited the disciples to touch his hands and his feet and asked them to cook him some fish. They stared at him as he ate. They couldn't believe their eyes.

Jesus stayed on earth with them for 40 days before going back to heaven. He spent a great deal of time talking about the Kingdom. He had begun his ministry by proclaiming news of the Kingdom, and he ended it the same way.

The disciples were ready to see Jesus bring the Kingdom right then. They were anxious to see the world brought under control. "So when the apostles were with Jesus, they kept asking him, "Lord, has the time come for you to free Israel and restore our kingdom?"" (Acts 1:6 NLT).

"He replied, 'The Father alone has the authority to set those dates and times, and they are not for you to know'" (Acts 1:7 NLT). It was not up to them to know the dates of his return. Neither is it up to us. Their responsibility then and ours today is to be witnesses of Jesus and his coming Kingdom.

Before Jesus left, he told them they must go to Jerusalem and wait for the Helper he would send. Even though he was leaving, someone else was coming. He would empower his people to be his witnesses. "But you will receive power when the Holy Spirit comes upon you. And you will be my witnesses, telling people about me everywhere—in Jerusalem, throughout Judea, in Samaria, and to the ends of the earth" (Acts 1:8 NLT).

After he reiterated their mission, he left. He ascended to the other world in a cloud. The disciples must have lingered a while. Two angels came to those who were left standing there. "Men of Galilee," they said, "why are you standing here staring into heaven? Jesus has been taken from you into heaven, but someday he will return from heaven in the same way you saw him go!" (Acts 1:11 NLT). Stop staring and go! They left for Jerusalem and waited for the Helper Jesus had promised.

Part 3
GETTING HELP

Chapter 11

THE HELPER COMES

I have wondered what it would have been like to be there when Jesus raised Lazarus from the dead. Or to see him touch a blind man's eyes and give him sight. To marvel as he healed a paralytic. I would have wanted Jesus to stay and not leave this earth. I would have asked him to heal all the sick. Raise all the dead. Run for office. Take control of this out-of-control world right now!

The disciples didn't want Jesus to go either. I can't blame them. Surprisingly, Jesus told them it was better if he left.

"Nevertheless, I tell you the truth: it is to your advantage that I go away, for if I do not go away, the Helper will not come to you. But if I go, I will send him to you" (John 16:7 NLT).

I imagine the disciples scratched their heads as Jesus uttered those words. It must have seemed strange for Jesus to say that it was better if he went away. They didn't understand it then, but later it would make sense.

While Jesus was on earth, he could only be in one place at one time. The Helper, that is the Holy Spirit, whom Jesus promised to send, wasn't limited by geographical space or distance. He could be with many people at once. He could be wherever his followers were. He could help them by filling them and giving them supernatural power.

While the Helper brings power to Jesus' followers, he shouldn't be understood as just a "power" or "force" in the universe. He is not a Jedi. He is God, one of the distinct persons of the Trinity. Dr. Wayne Grudem defines the Trinity this way: "God eternally exists as three persons, Father, Son, and Holy Spirit (the Helper), and each person is fully God, and there is one God."[15]

A prophecy was made thousands of years ago that the Holy Spirit would be poured out on God's people in the later days.

"I will pour out my Spirit upon all people. Your sons and daughters will prophesy. Your old men will dream dreams, and your young men will see visions. In those days I will pour out my Spirit even on servants—men and women alike" (Joel 2:28-29 NLT).

In the time before Jesus, only certain people, such as anointed rulers and prophets, experienced the indwelling power of the Holy Spirit. But in the last days, the age after Jesus' resurrection, all of God's people from the least to the greatest would experience it.

In the Old Covenant, God wrote his commandments on stone tablets. But in the New Covenant, the Holy Spirit would write his laws on the hearts and minds of God's people.

With his laws written on our hearts and minds, we are able to carry out the will of God in a way that people before Jesus couldn't. Where they had to go to a temple or sanctuary to experience God's Spirit, we can experience God's Spirit wherever we are. We have become the Spirit's sanctuary. Now we have the opportunity to experience a closeness and intimacy that didn't exist for everyone before the

Spirit was poured out. He speaks to us, reminds us of things, and empowers us in a personal way.

It began as the first followers of Jesus waited in Jerusalem on the day of Pentecost, the Jewish holiday celebrating the end of the grain harvest. They waited just as Jesus and the angel had commanded them. It was 9 in the morning. It had been 50 days since Jesus was crucified. There was anticipation in the air and probably a lot of second guessing.

Then it happened. "Suddenly, there was a sound from heaven like the roaring of a mighty windstorm, and it filled the house where they were sitting" (Acts 1:2 NLT).

The sound of wind announced the coming of the Spirit. That was appropriate. You can't see the wind, but you can see its effects. In the same way, you can't see the Spirit but you can see evidence of his presence. And just as with the wind, there is mystery to the working of the Holy Spirit. He blows where and when he chooses.

He filled the house and those in it that day. As the Holy Spirit was poured out on them, the disciples were filled, empowered, and given the supernatural ability to speak in unlearned languages.

Those who witnessed this filling thought the disciples were drunk. Peter, now empowered with the boldness of the Holy Spirit, stepped up and explained to the crowd what was happening.

"Listen carefully, all of you, fellow Jews and residents of Jerusalem! Make no mistake about this. These people are not drunk, as some of you are assuming. Nine o'clock in the morning is much too early for that" (Acts 2:14b-15 NLT).

He explained that everyone present was witnessing the fulfillment of the prophecy from the Scriptures. He invited the people to repent and turn to God and be baptized. If they did, they, too, would receive the gift of the promised Helper.

They wanted what they had just witnessed. 3,000 people were so moved that morning that they were baptized immediately in the name of Jesus. Then they, too, received the gift of the Holy Spirit. What they received is available to all of us today. If we repent and turn to God for salvation, we will receive new life and the gift of the Spirit.

The Helper Gives New Life

The process of receiving new life that the Spirit gives is called being "born again" or "born from above".[16] The phrase "born from above" carries the idea of spiritual rebirth from the other world, from heaven. Jesus said you can't see the Kingdom unless you are born again (John 3:3 NLT). To enter heaven requires a new spiritual birth that only the Holy Spirit can give.

It is an act of God and initiated by God. "They are reborn—not with a physical birth resulting from human passion or plan, but a birth that comes from God" (John 1:13 NLT).

We were born with spiritual blindness. We can't understand the things of the Spirit until we are born again. This spiritual blindness is part of the deception that started at the beginning when Satan deceived Adam and Eve. Satan became the god of this world and blinded our spiritual eyes (2 Corinthians 4:4 NLT).

When you are born again, a whole new world is opened to you. You see and understand spiritual things you couldn't before. When people sing, "I was blind, but now I see," that is the experience they are describing. Because of the outpouring of the Holy Spirit, they can see and understand the things of the Spirit in a way they couldn't before. The phenomenon is similar to what a blind person would experience if he miraculously received sight.

Nicodemus, a religious leader of his day, was trying to understand all of this. He was confused and asked Jesus to further explain what it meant to be born again.

"What do you mean?" exclaimed Nicodemus. "How can an old man go back into his mother's womb and be born again?" (John 3:4 NLT).

Jesus told him, "Humans can reproduce only human life, but the Holy Spirit gives birth to spiritual life" (John 3:6 NLT).

Jesus wanted Nicodemus to understand that spiritual life can only be given by the Spirit of God. Being born again is a spiritual regeneration in which God imparts new life to us.

The transformation is similar to the metamorphosis undergone by a caterpillar that enters a chrysalis and comes out a butterfly. When you metamorphosize by the power of God, your identity and nature are changed. You become a new person. You become something much better than what you were before. A new life begins for you.

"This means that anyone who belongs to Christ has become a new person. The old life is gone; a new life has begun!" (2 Corinthians 5:17 NLT).

I was 19 when I received this new life. Before it happened, I was unsettled and unsatisfied, searching for help.

Late one night, I went with a friend, Scott Korey, to go watch planes take off and land at a small airport near my house. We went to watch the planes, but we also went to talk about our lives. I was searching for answers, trying to make sense out of life.

We smoked Marlboros in his beat-up Chevy Chevette as we talked. All of sudden, I was overcome with the feeling that a spiritual presence was there. I didn't hear the sound of a mighty windstorm like the early disciples did, but I knew there was an awakening happening inside of me. It was hard to explain.

I turned to my friend and told him that I felt like someone else was in the car with us. Looking back now, I know what was happening. The Holy Spirit had blown in like a rushing wind. I was being born from above, experiencing a spiritual rebirth. My eyes were being opened.

I prayed a short, unreligious prayer that night in response to the Spirit's prompting. I think it went something like, "God, I have made a mess of my life so far. Please take my life and do something with it". I asked him to take control, and when I did, I was flooded with an overwhelming peace. I felt new. I asked for forgiveness and gave my life to him. What happened that night changed me forever. I was born again.

It is rare that two people have the same experience. Everyone's is a little different, but the results are the same. When we are born again, we become new creations with new power to help us live life in this out-of-control world. It is for that purpose that the Spirit came.

Chapter 12
THE HELPER EMPOWERS US

That day was the beginning of a new journey for me, a spiritual journey I am still on to this day. I had a new sense of purpose and power in my life. I had a peace and assurance I had never experienced. That is part of what the Holy Spirit does.

He is a down payment in our here and now for what is yet to come. He indwells us, and he doesn't leave.

The Scriptures speak of two different things he does for us indwelling and filling. There are differences between the two. The *indwelling of the Holy Spirit* is a *one-time experience* for all believers in Christ. You are indwelt with the Spirit when you repent of your sins and place your faith in Jesus for salvation. That is a promise to all who trust in him. You are indwelt, sealed, and joined with God's Spirit once.

The *filling of the Spirit*, on the other hand, is a *recurring experience* for all believers in Christ. While we are indwelt once, we are filled over and over again, day by day, moment by moment, in every situation.

The Helper Fills Us

To be filled with the Spirit is to be controlled by him. It means we give up being controlled by our natural desires and the world to let the Spirit control and guide us. When we are filled with the Spirit, we allow God to direct our thoughts, attitudes, and actions.

The Apostle Paul said, "Don't be drunk with wine, because that will ruin your life. Instead, *be filled with the Holy Spirit*" (Ephesians 5:18 NLT).

While being filled means you are controlled by the Spirit, he doesn't force you to do things against your will. He will speak to you and prompt you, but he won't overrule your will. You have to choose to yield your will to his. When you do, he will help you grow spiritually and enable you to take on new roles and assignments from God.

In the early church, people were chosen for certain roles because they were filled with the Holy Spirit on an ongoing basis. People like Stephen. He was placed in charge of a ministry caring for the poor because others recognized that he was full of the Spirit. He continued to do greater things, teaching and preaching the gospel with boldness. He preached with such boldness that he angered a group of Jewish leaders on one fateful day. They were so angry that they dragged him out of the city to stone him to death.

Even in his final moments, he was still filled with the Spirit. He saw heaven open, and he gazed into the other world. He saw Jesus standing beside his Heavenly Father. And then he prayed that God wouldn't hold the sin against the men who were taking his life. He became the first martyr of the Christian faith. The Holy Spirit is the one who helped Stephen demonstrate such great love, faith, and boldness in the midst of hate and persecution.

There are other stories in the Bible in which the filling of the Spirit gave someone a supernatural dose of power to accomplish something they couldn't do in their own strength. Gideon defeated an army of several hundred thousand with only 300 men. Samson killed a thousand men with a jawbone. A young David killed Goliath with a sling and some stones. Peter preached to thousands on the day of Pentecost and 3,000 people were baptized in the name of Jesus. There are other examples of people speaking in unknown languages, doing miraculous works, and doing menial tasks with supernatural passion and energy because of the empowerment of the Holy Spirit. The Spirit fills us so we can accomplish things of eternal value.

That brings up an important caution. People can mistakenly think that just because someone possesses charisma, has excellent communication skills, or is gifted with special musical abilities, they must be filled with the Holy Spirit. Don't be misled by talent and charisma. Don't assume that a person is Spirit-filled because they are a gifted speaker or singer. Talent and ability don't necessarily mean that someone is filled with the Spirit.

For example, some people in the Bible were filled with the Spirit and yet were not talented communicators. Neither Moses nor Paul were gifted speakers, but God filled them and used them to accomplish incredible things for his Kingdom. Moses wrote the majority of the Old Testament, and Paul wrote the majority of the New Testament.

Moses led over a million slaves out of Egypt, watched God split the Red Sea, and received the Ten Commandments, but he got tongue-tied.

Paul planted hundreds of churches and has impacted millions of people through his writings in the New Testament, but people were not impressed with him in person and often fell asleep during his preaching.

So don't equate talent or charisma with being Spirit-filled. Character trumps charisma every time.

To receive the power of the Holy Spirit, we have to depend on God's power and not our own. Pride and self-reliance will quench the work of the Spirit. Being filled with the Spirit requires dependence on God and not on our own abilities. Our part is to completely rely on him. "It is not by force nor by strength, but by my Spirit, says the Lord of Heaven's Armies" (Zechariah 4:6 NLT).

Jesus compared this reliance on God to the dependence a branch must have on a grape vine to produce fruit. Jesus said, "Yes, I am the vine; you are the branches. Those who remain in me, and I in them, will produce much fruit. For apart from me you can do nothing" (John 15:5 NLT).

People who are genuinely filled with the Spirit will produce fruit that has lasting Kingdom results, fruit that expresses itself in love toward others. Those who do not stay connected can't produce anything of eternal value.

You depend on God to produce the fruit, but you still need to do your part. You are like a farmer. You have to cultivate the ground, plant the seeds, water the plants, and pull the weeds. Then you trust God to do his part. Ultimately it is up to him to produce the fruit. You need his grace in order to experience spiritual vitality and growth. You can't manufacture these things in yourself. You have to remain in him in order to see fruit.

When you remain in him, you will see the fruit of the Spirit produced in your life in increasing measure over time. The fruit of the Spirit is: "love, joy, peace, patience, kindness, goodness, faithfulness, gentleness, and self-control. There is no law against these things!" (Galatians 5:22-23 NLT).

To allow the Spirit to produce fruit in your life, you must let the Spirit fill you and guide you. Doing so requires a battle.

The Scriptures tell us that there are two forces battling within us, the desires of the Spirit and the desires of the sinful nature. They are constantly fighting for control.

George Bernard Shaw shared this illustration to explain the conflict: "A Native American Elder once described his own inner struggles in this manner: 'Inside of me there are two dogs. One of the dogs is mean and evil. The other dog is good. The mean dog fights the good dog all the time.' When asked which dog wins, he reflected for a moment and replied, 'The one I feed the most.'"[17]

The desire you feed will be the one that wins in you, too. You will have to starve the desires of your sinful nature if you want to be Spirit-filled. You will have to die to yourself. Sinful desires don't die easily. They don't go down without a fight. We must put effort into throwing off our sinful natures and clothing ourselves with our new Spirit-filled ones.

When you live according to the desires of your sinful nature, the results are "sexual immorality, impurity, lustful pleasures, idolatry, sorcery, hostility, quarreling, jealousy, outbursts of anger, selfish ambition, dissension, division, envy, drunkenness, wild parties, and other sins like these" (Galatians 5:19-21 NLT).

We must leave our former ways of life and embrace our new eternal lives. We must put lust and deception to death and let the Spirit renew our thoughts and attitudes. When we do, the Spirit will exchange the old for the new, swap the bad for the good. He will open our eyes, help us make the changes we need to make, and accomplish great things. It all begins in the heart.

Chapter 13

GUARDING YOUR HEART

The battle between the old and new natures happens in your heart. Your heart is the essence of who you are. It is your intellect, emotions, and will. It is where you think, feel, and decide. Jesus said, "For from the heart come evil thoughts, murder, adultery, all sexual immorality, theft, lying, and slander" (Matthew 15:19 NLT).

What goes on inside of you will eventually come out. The greatest acts of love and kindness began in human hearts, as did the worst atrocities. That is why the Scriptures admonish you to, "Guard your heart above all else, for it determines the course of your life" (Proverbs 4:23 NLT).

How do you guard your heart? You pay attention to it. You watch it. You listen to it. That way you can help redirect it when it wanders.

We all tend to wander. Our hearts wander. Our minds wander. There is an old hymn that says, "Prone to wander, Lord, I feel it. Prone to leave the God I love. Here's my heart, Lord. Take and seal it."[4]

---

[4] Come, Thou Fount of Every Blessing

When we wander, we stray from a path. Just as a ship can drift off course if not navigated intentionally, our lives can drift from the course God has set for us. None of us are immune.

A wandering heart looks for ways to escape and numb the pain of a broken world. It seeks out pleasure, people, and possessions to make it feel better. It may lead you to go on a shopping spree and spend more than you can afford, to drink too much, or to put too much pressure on someone in your life to meet your needs.

You also need to guard your heart from becoming hardened. The brokenness of this world can create callouses if you let it. Your heart can become impenetrable from bitterness. It can become rigid from pride. When it is hardened, you won't be able to hear the Holy Spirit speaking to you.

People with hardened hearts blame others for their problems. They blame parents, spouses, bosses, the government. Jesus said when you cast blame, you ignore the problems in your own life that are often much bigger. "And why worry about a speck in your friend's eye when you have a log in your own?" (Matthew 7:3 NLT).

In your heart there is a throne of control. Whoever or whatever is on that throne will rule your life. You alone have the ability to decide who will reign. God created this place in your heart so that he could rule and reign. That is why Jesus said the most important commandment is to "love the Lord your God with all your heart, all your soul, and all your mind" (Matthew 22:37 NLT).

Whatever or whoever you love will reign on the throne of your heart. When you love God with all of your heart, he will rule and reign, and good things will flow out. When you allow self to rule and reign on the throne, bad things will flow out.

Self wants control of the throne, and he will fight for it. Because self is used to being king, he won't come off the throne easily. He wants to be noticed, praised, and fed. When self stays on the throne, his goal is to feed the desires of the flesh. Two of those desires are the lust for sex outside of marriage and the love of money.

Sexual Immorality

It is important to understand that sex is beautiful as God designed it. Sex was created to be the expression of a one-flesh relationship between a husband and wife, and it should be enjoyed in this context. It is a celebration of oneness, unity, and pleasure. God created sex with a practical purpose as well - to enable his creation to be fruitful and multiply.

Sex is a sacred gift, and it should be protected. The Scriptures say, "Drink water from your own well— share your love only with your wife. Why spill the water of your springs in the streets, having sex with just anyone? You should reserve it for yourselves. Never share it with strangers. Let your wife be a fountain of blessing for you. Rejoice in the wife of your youth. She is a loving deer, a graceful doe. Let her breasts satisfy you always. May you always be captivated by her love" (Proverbs 5:15-19 NLT).

While this is the ideal for sex, the world and our natures are broken. You and I were born with broken sexual desires. Each of us has a tendency to gravitate toward some kind of sexual impurity. Our brokenness is expressed in different ways. Satan knows this and attacks this area of our lives.

Satan wants to take something God intended for good and pervert it. He knows the power it has to throw our lives further out of control. He uses the powerful temptation of sex outside of marriage to entrap us. He says, "Why wait?", or "You love each other, so it's OK", or

"You deserve to be happy." He promotes forbidden pleasure just as he did in the Garden.

But unlike God-given pleasures that satisfy, the forbidden pleasures Satan offers are short-lived. They leave you feeling empty rather than full. Satan uses the temptation of short-lived sinful pleasure to accomplish his mission to steal, kill, and destroy all that is good in your life.

Sexual immorality leads to greater hurt and chaos in our world. Rape, abuse, sex trafficking, and pornography all abuse the gift of sex. Sexual immorality always hurts others. Sexual abuse can ruin the lives of its victims. Pornography causes millions of people, men and women, to feel defeated in their daily lives and negatively affects their relationships, self-images, and how they view others.

All types of sexual immorality affect people deeply. The Scriptures tell us that sexual immorality is unique in comparison to all other sins. "No other sin so clearly affects the body as this one does. For sexual immorality is a sin against your own body" (1 Corinthians 6:18b NLT). You hurt yourself when you engage in any kind of sexual immorality.

When you are indwelt by the Spirit, you gain a power you didn't have previously to overcome sexual temptation. You no longer have to be a slave to your out-of-control sexual desires. In Christ, you have been set free, and the Holy Spirit is here to help you. Although you are free, the battle continues, and there are some practical tactics you should use in the face of sexual temptation.

Run from Sexual Sin!

The Apostle Paul said emphatically, "Run from sexual sin!" (I Corinthians 6:18a NLT). While most temptation requires resistance to overcome, sexual temptation is best overcome by running away from it. Your best defense is to flee. Although fleeing is the exact opposite of what your flesh may feel like doing, it is wise to run in the opposite direction as far and as fast as you can. Don't try to stand there and fight it. Get out of the situation as quickly as possible.

That is exactly what Joseph did. The Bible says, "Joseph was a very handsome and well-built young man" (Genesis 39:6 NLT). Joseph had been put in charge of the house of Potiphar, an officer of the Pharaoh in Egypt.

Potiphar had a wife. As she began to notice Joseph's good looks and well-built physique, her desires for him grew. Eventually, she demanded that he come and sleep with her.

Joseph could have enjoyed a few moments of sinful pleasure. It is possible that no one else would ever have known. But he wisely refused her advances out of respect for God's commands and for her husband.

He told her, "My master trusts me with everything in his entire household. No one here has more authority than I do. He has held back nothing from me except you, because you are his wife. How could I do such a wicked thing? It would be a great sin against God" (Genesis 39:8-9 NLT).

Still, she wanted to sleep with him. His response may have made her want him more. She didn't stop her sexual advances. He kept refusing. He tried to avoid her. "She kept putting pressure on Joseph day after day, but he refused to sleep with her, and he kept out of her way as much as possible" (Genesis 39:10 NLT).

She had become obsessed with her sexual desire. Out-of-control sexual desires will lead you to push the limits and throw caution to the wind.

"One day, however, no one else was around when he went in to do his work. She came and grabbed him by his cloak, demanding, "Come on, sleep with me!" Joseph tore himself away, but he left his cloak in her hand as he ran from the house" (Genesis 39:11-12 NLT).

Joseph did the only thing he could. He looked for the way out and ran. The Holy Spirit will always help you find a way out. He will show you the "Exit" sign. Joseph saw it and ran toward it. He did the right thing and fled.

Potiphar's wife was angry. She was humiliated. So she falsely accused him. Her accusations landed him in prison, but while others doubted his innocence, God knew the truth.

God sees all things. He saw Joseph's integrity. While those in charge sentenced him, God commended him. That commendation eventually led to his freedom. After a couple of years, Joseph was released from prison and appointed to the position of prime minister by Pharaoh. His situation was completely reversed, from prison to palace.

Joseph's decision to run away from sexual temptation revealed his character and was one of the reasons God gave him a bigger assignment. Joseph probably wouldn't have been appointed to such a powerful position if he hadn't fled that day. God often permits difficult circumstances to come into our lives in order to test our character and see what we can be entrusted with. When it comes to sexual temptation, the proper response is to run.

You may not have to run out the door like Joseph did when fleeing sexual temptation. Your battle may require subtler tactics. In their book *Every Man's Battle: Winning the War on Sexual Temptation One Victory at a Time,* Steve Arterburn and Fred Stoeker share a practical way in which you can flee visual sexual temptation. They recommend "bouncing the eyes."

"The problem is that your eyes have always bounced toward the sexual, and you've made no attempt to end this habit. To combat it, you need to build a reflex action by training your eyes to immediately bounce away from the sexual, like the jerk of your hand away from a hot stove."[18]

You may need to retrain yourself to bounce your eyes. You may need to put software on your computer or phone to block pornography. You may need to shut down an email account or social media account. Do whatever it takes to run from sexual temptation. The Holy Spirit will help you. He is always there and willing to help you find a way out when tempted.

Have Frequent Sex

The Apostle Paul wrote to correct the misunderstanding that sex of any kind, even within marriage, should be avoided. He explained that one of the most practical ways to combat sexual temptation is for married couples to have regular, frequent, and consensual sex. According to Paul, marriage is THE place for sexuality. "But because there is so much sexual immorality, each man should have his own wife, and each woman should have her own husband" (1 Corinthians 7:2 NLT).

Frequent sex within marriage reduces the temptation for sexual sin because it meets your desire for sex the way God intended. Paul goes on to explain the need for frequent sex.

"Do not deprive each other of sexual relations, unless you both agree to refrain from sexual intimacy for a limited time so you can give yourselves more completely to prayer. Afterward, you should come together again so that Satan won't be able to tempt you because of your lack of self-control" (1 Corinthians 7:5 NLT).

A husband or wife who denies his or her spouse regular sex is placing him or her in a difficult position. There is an overwhelming amount of sexual temptation around us. Husbands and wives must help each other resist by meeting each other's sexual needs.

Lack of frequent sex in marriage is a major factor leading to extra-marital affairs, and while it doesn't justify them, it does address a simple truth. If needs are not met at home, the enemy is ready to tempt husbands and wives to meet those needs outside of the marriage relationship.

So how often should married couples have sex? The Bible doesn't say, but it does make it clear that married couples should only withhold sex from one another if there is mutual agreement. This means there needs to be honest discussion and agreement about the frequency of sex in marriage to ensure that each partner's needs are being met. When needs are met, it helps diffuse the temptation for sexual immorality.

It has been my experience in working with couples that people who are more content and sexually fulfilled in their marriage are more fulfilled in other areas of their life, too.

I have also found that husbands and wives don't typically have the same sex drives. In a relationship, one person's drive is usually stronger than the other's. If your drive is lower than your spouse's drive, remember that his or her sex drive is good and was placed there by God. To ignore it or hope it goes away is not the right approach. Rather, you should be committed to meeting your spouse's needs.

The Single Person and Sex

So where does that leave the single person? If sex was created only to be part of the marriage relationship, then what is a single person to do? John Piper says first we need to understand that the "sexual desire of the unmarried person is good, is holy, and is part of the shining creation of the image of God."[18] Your sexual desires are God-given. They are part of what leads you to want to be married.

Still, trying to follow God's plan as you wait can be challenging to say the least. There are many temptations to have sex outside of marriage. What you need to know is that learning to combat sexual temptations as a single person *now* is great preparation for marriage *later*. In marriage, you will continue to face sexual temptation. It doesn't magically go away. You will be tempted to have sex with someone other than your spouse. You will go through seasons with little or no sex and have to wrestle with unmet sexual desires. How you handle the waiting and temptations now will help prepare you to be a faithful spouse later on.

Also, in some situations, God grants the gift of singleness and celibacy. That was the case for the Apostle Paul. "But I wish everyone were single, just as I am. Yet each person has a special gift from God, of one kind or another" (1 Corinthians 7:7 NLT). Paul was content to remain unmarried. Jesus was, too. God gives some people a gift of contentment in their singleness.

Each of us is unique, and each of us needs to follow the call God places on our lives when it comes to marriage and singleness. The married person should not look down on the single person or think something is wrong with him or her and vice versa. Each person should do what God has called him or her to do in each season of life.

Will God Give You More Than You Can Handle?

As you wrestle with your desires and temptations, it is important to know that God won't allow you to experience temptation beyond what you can stand.

Some people have misunderstood this promise, applying it to trials instead of temptations. They say, "God won't give you more than you can handle." To make it worse, they say it, with good intentions, to people who have lost their jobs, experienced a loss, or encountered a difficult situation. Rather than helping, this "encouragement" often leads to frustration for the people to whom it is given.

This misuse of the promise comes from the following verse:

"The temptations in your life are no different from what others experience. And God is faithful. He will not allow the temptation to be more than you can stand. When you are tempted, he will show you a way out so that you can endure" (1 Corinthians 10:13 NLT).

The promise isn't that God won't give you more than you can handle in regards to trials, but that he won't allow you to face temptations beyond what you can handle.

God will often allow you to go through painful situations that break you. He will allow you to go through difficulties that are more than you can handle by yourself. He does this so you will learn to depend on him.

He promises to walk with you through every difficult season of life. He promises not to leave you. He promises a way out if you are tempted by sin, but he doesn't promise to remove you from trials, tribulations, and difficult times.

God uses the trials in your life to grow your faith. James, the brother of Jesus, wrote, "Dear brothers and sisters, when troubles of any kind come your way, consider it an opportunity for great joy. For you know that when your faith is tested, your endurance has a chance to grow. So let it grow, for when your endurance is fully developed, you will be perfect and complete, needing nothing" (James 1:2-4 NLT).

You should lean into trials and look for the way of escape when tempted. Accept trials as God's strength and conditioning program. Embrace them. Allow endurance to grow, even when it must grow through pain. Don't bail out. Let God do the work he needs to do as he builds the muscles of your faith. And look for the way out when tempted, knowing that God won't allow you to be tempted beyond what you can bear.

Confession

In an ideal world, we would never sin. But the reality is that all of us have and all of us will. It could be a lustful thought or an action based on that thought. The good news is that there is forgiveness when we sin. To access God's forgiveness, all we have to do is confess our sin to God.

The Scriptures tell us, "But if we confess our sins to him, he is faithful and just to forgive us our sins and to cleanse us from all wickedness" (1 John 1:9 NLT).

When we confess our sins to God, he promises to forgive and cleanse us. Confession is like soap for your soul. It cleans you on the inside.

That is what King David experienced after committing adultery with Bathsheba. David hid his sin for a while. He didn't confess it to God or others and simply went on his way. Then Nathan the prophet, prompted by God, confronted David about his sexual sin. Once his sin was exposed, David confessed it to God.

That is often a pattern with sexual sin. People keep it secret for as long as possible and only come clean once it is somehow disclosed. That is not the best way. No sin can be kept hidden forever. At some point, it will be revealed.

Jesus said, "The time is coming when everything that is covered up will be revealed, and all that is secret will be made known to all. Whatever you have said in the dark will be heard in the light, and what you have whispered behind closed doors will be shouted from the housetops for all to hear!" (Luke 12:2-3 NLT).

Dealing with our sin in immediate, humble, private confession before God is better than dealing with it much later through public confession in disgrace. That is where the Holy Spirit helps. He will search your heart as you allow him, revealing areas that need attention and praying for you when you don't know what to say.

After King David's sin was made known, he asked for God to forgive and cleanse him. He prayed, "Have mercy on me, O God, because of your unfailing love. Because of your great compassion, blot out the stain of my sins. Wash me clean from my guilt. Purify me from my sin" (Psalm 51:1-2 NLT).

David asked God to clean him from the inside out because sexual sin makes you feel dirty. It muddies your heart and soul.

Confession cleanses your soul. It's like washing dirty clothes. Stinky, mud-stained garments go into the washer, and fresh-smelling, clean clothes come out. In the same way, our dirty, stinky sin gets washed by the blood of Christ, and we come out white as snow. Your dirty laundry won't get clean unless you wash it, and your sins won't be removed unless you confess them. The same is true of your heart. You have to ask God to purify you. When you do, he will.

When you sin sexually, there may be others to whom you need to confess your sin after you have confessed it to God. Your spouse. Your children. Other people you may have hurt. In the case of a sexual crime, you will have to face criminal consequences. You need to understand that it will take time to heal the hurt caused by your sin in other people's lives. God's forgiveness comes instantly, but it will take time to earn the trust of others again.

That was the case for a husband and wife who came to visit my office. After brief introductions, I asked them what had brought them in to see me. They explained that there had been an affair. The husband had cheated on his wife and had confessed it to her the week before. He felt better after confessing and was ready to move forward.

The wife, on the other hand, was dealing with the reality of what he had done. She was devastated. She had lots of questions that he needed to answer. He didn't feel like answering them. I explained that he would have to. He wanted me to help her move on. I wanted to help him slow down and work through the process of regaining her trust.

I explained to the husband that the recovery process would take a long time. While he had moved on past the difficulty of confessing his sin, her difficulty was just beginning. I told him that if their marriage was to be restored, his actions moving forward would have to demonstrate that he could be trusted. It could take a year, two years, three, or longer. He had to rebuild what he had damaged. God's forgiveness had come to him instantly, but regaining his wife's trust would be a process.

The same goes for any of us who sin sexually. There are consequences. It will take time to rebuild trust. For a pastor, or volunteer in a church, it could mean removal from his or her role while they get help and work on their marriage. For a spouse it could mean new boundaries concerning where he or she goes, whom he or she hangs out with, and his or her involvement with social media. There are steps that have to be taken in order to rebuild trust.

If you know someone who has sinned sexually, it is your responsibility to respond to him or her with humility and grace. You can help restore them if they invite you into that process. If they don't, you can pray for them from a distance. Either way, you should stay humble as you interact with people whose sexual sins have been exposed. Remember the old adage, "There but by the grace of God go I." Recognize that you, too, are susceptible to temptation and sin.

Remember that Jesus will use the same standards to judge you by which you judge others. If you are harsh in judging others, he will be harsh in judging you. If you are gentle, he will be gentle. "For you will be treated as you treat others. The standard you use in judging is the standard by which you will be judged" (Matthew 7:1-2 NLT).

The Love of Money

Another prominent sin our sinful nature tends to gravitate toward is the love of money. Some think the Bible says that "money is the root of evil." That, however, is not true. Money is neutral; it has no moral value. The Scriptures say, "For the love of money is the root of all kinds of evil. And some people, craving money, have wandered from the true faith and pierced themselves with many sorrows" (1 Timothy 6:10 NLT).

Money is not the root of evil. It is the *love* of money that causes problems. The love of money is linked to what the Scriptures call idolatry, putting money or material things before God.

Jesus addressed the problem our hearts have with idolatry and money. "No one can serve two masters. For you will hate one and love the other; you will be devoted to one and despise the other. You cannot serve God and be enslaved to money" (Matthew 6:24 NLT).

The love of money will control you if you let it. It can be a subtle process, but over time money will become an idol for you if you don't guard your heart. Your heart can easily become enamored with the luxuries and comfort of life that money provides. We begin to love what it provides and seek more of it. It becomes an insatiable desire. Before we realize it, we may be seeking it and relying on it more than we seek and rely on God.

God knew we would struggle with this in a broken world. To keep money from having too much control over you, he asks you to keep your hands open instead of closed. He asks you to be generous with what you have. He wants you to realize that he is in control of all that you have. He is the owner, and you are the manager. That is why he asks you to give. Give to your church. Give to those in need. Give to a stranger. Be generous.

When a rich young ruler came to Jesus asking what he needed to do to inherit eternal life, Jesus told him he needed to first sell all he had and give it to the poor and afterward to come follow him. The rich young ruler looked down. That was too much to ask. He couldn't give up all his possessions. His hands were closed. He refused Jesus' offer and walked away. Not only were his hands closed, but his heart was closed, too.

In contrast, Jesus praised a poor widow. She opened her hands and put two small coins in the collection box at the temple. The rich put in large amounts, giving out of their abundance, but she gave out of her poverty. Jesus said, "For they gave a tiny part of their surplus, but she, poor as she is, has given everything she had to live on" (Mark 12:44 NLT). Her hands were open and her heart was open.

The irony is that a rich person can be dissatisfied in wealth while a poor person can be content in poverty. The secret to contentment is not found in how much you acquire and keep. The secret to contentment is found in being satisfied with what God provides. That kind of contentment is learned. The Apostle Paul said, "Not that I was ever in need, for I have learned how to be content with whatever I have" (Philippians 4:11 NLT).

One thing that will help you learn contentment is having an eternal perspective about your possessions. An eternal perspective helps remind you that you can't take your earthly possessions to heaven when you die. They stay behind.

It also reminds you that you can store up heavenly possessions through deposits you make in the here and now. Jesus said, "Don't store up treasures here on earth, where moths eat them and rust destroys them, and where thieves break in and steal. Store your treasures in heaven, where moths and rust cannot destroy, and thieves do not break in and steal. Wherever your treasure is, there the desires of your heart will also be" (Matthew 6:19-21 NLT).

If you want to know what the desires of your heart are, follow the money trail. Where you spend and invest your money is where your heart will be drawn. If your money goes only to things of this world, your heart will be here. If a portion of your money goes to eternal, heavenly things, your heart will be there. God wants to help break your fixation on the temporary by having you invest your money in the eternal. You will lose everything in the temporal, but your investments in eternal things will last forever.

As you learn to invest in eternal things, temporary things tend to lose their tight grip on your heart. Every time you give financially to a church, a person in need, or an organization that impacts people's lives for God, you weaken money's power in your life. Investing in eternal things redirects your heart to the proper place, helping you prioritize the things of God.

What you do with the things entrusted to you in the here and now will determine what is entrusted to you in the "not yet." In the here and now, we are all entrusted with different amounts. It doesn't matter how much or how little God entrusts to you. What matters is what you do with it. God entrusts you with wealth and possessions and expects you to invest them for his Kingdom's sake.

He doesn't want you to worry about the things you need in the here and now either. He promises to provide those things for you as you seek him. Jesus said, "Seek the Kingdom of God above all else, and he will give you everything you need" (Luke 12:31 NLT).

The Holy Spirit wants to help you on this journey. If you are going to let the Spirit renew your heart, then you will have to listen to him, yield to him, and do what he leads you to do. It all begins with listening. In order to listen, you need to know how he speaks to you. He speaks through the Scriptures, through inner promptings, and through other people.

Chapter 14

THE HELPER SPEAKS TO YOU

The Holy Spirit primarily speaks to you through the Scriptures. He will never contradict what is revealed there. That is because he inspired people to write them. They are his words.

"Above all, you must realize that no prophecy in Scripture ever came from the prophet's own understanding, or from human initiative. No, those prophets were moved by the Holy Spirit, and they spoke from God" (2 Peter 1:20-21 NLT).

The people who wrote the books of the Bible were inspired by the Holy Spirit. The words of the Bible are Holy-Spirit-breathed words. The Spirit will illuminate these words for you, opening your spiritual eyes so you can understand spiritual truths. He will help you see how to apply those truths to your life.

He has done that for me over and over. I can remember one time vividly. I was 19 and trying to determine if I should go to college. I felt like God wanted me to go, but I didn't know how I could afford it. I didn't know if I would be accepted. I hadn't taken college prep classes in high school, and wondered if I had missed my chance. I knelt by my bed one night and prayed. I asked God to help me, to show me what to do. Then into my mind came the words "Proverbs 3:5-6." I was a new Christian and had never read that passage before.

I got up from praying and picked up my Bible. I turned to the book of Proverbs and read, "Trust in the Lord with all your heart; do not depend on your own understanding. Seek his will in all you do, and he will show you which path to take" (Proverbs 3:5-6 NLT). The Holy Spirit revealed those verses to me and gave me assurance with his peace that everything was going to work out. I only needed to trust in God with all my heart.

Within the next few weeks, I was accepted to a college near my home. I received a grant that paid for all my tuition and all my books. God not only opened the doors for me to attend college but also paid the way. That was where he wanted me to be.

I connected with a small Christian organization on campus that helped disciple me in my faith. I met my wife there. I earned my degree. My decision to lean on God instead of my own understanding made all the difference. God spoke to me through the Scriptures and made my path straight. I have seen the same thing play out again and again in my life.

In order to hear from God through the Scriptures, you need to read them on a regular basis. I encourage you to use a systematic reading plan to take you through the Scriptures. The website and app https://www.youversion.com/ has various reading plans from which you can choose. The more you read, the more you will recognize the Holy Spirit's voice.

The Holy Spirit Speaks Through Inner Promptings

The Holy Spirit will also speak to your spirit through inner promptings. You may experience these promptings as a spiritual nudge in your spirit leading you to take a step of faith for Jesus. One time I heard Pastor Andy Stanley say that we should "pay attention to the tension." That's good advice. If you are feeling uneasy, unsure, or unsettled about something, it could be the nudge of the Spirit trying to help you. Pay attention to those inner promptings.

The Spirit could be leading you to take an action, share an encouraging word or a word of rebuke, or pray a prayer. Each time you respond to the promptings of the Spirit, you will get better at recognizing his voice and direction in your life.

Dawn, a single mom on a limited income, told me that one morning she was going through the drive-through at a local coffee shop. She was pulling up to the window to pay for her order when the Spirit prompted her to pay for the person behind her in line. She did what she felt God prompting her to do and went on her way to work, not knowing why the Spirit had led her to perform this act of kindness.

Later at work, she told someone about her experience. That person said, "I think you paid for Sherry's order." Dawn was surprised. Sherry was her co-worker. Later, Sherry confirmed that she had indeed been the recipient of Dawn's act of kindness. Sherry explained that she had forgot her purse on the way to work and hadn't realized it until she pulled up to the window to pay for her drink. That was when the worker told her that her order had been paid for by the person in front of her. Sherry was pleasantly surprised. As she drove off, she thanked God for his provision. God providentially orchestrated things for both of them that morning.

Sherry was amazed that God would concern himself with such a small detail as a morning cup of coffee, that he would prompt another person to bless her unexpectedly. As Dawn and Sherry shared their story, it reminded them both how much God cares about the smallest things in our lives. The Scriptures say he knows the very number of hairs on our heads. He even knows when a sparrow falls to the ground. He cares about the small details of our lives. Dawn and Sherry can share their story today because Dawn followed the prompting of the Spirit.

I have experienced countless promptings by the Spirit in my own life over the years. He has prompted me to say something to someone or hold my tongue, to go somewhere or not go somewhere, to take a job or turn down a job, to reconcile a broken relationship or establish boundaries in a harmful one. In order to be filled by the Spirit, you must pay attention to his unique promptings in your life. You walk in the Spirit when you do what he leads you to do.

While the Spirit may prompt you to do things that take you out of your comfort zone, it is important to remember that he will never prompt you do anything that goes against what is written in the Scriptures. The Scriptures always trump any prompting or desire.

For example, a lady once told me that she was being led by God to leave her husband for another man. When I asked her how she knew God was telling her to do that, she said because, "God wants me to be happy." That was not a prompting from the Holy Spirit. It was a voice and desire that came from her own heart. Our hearts can't always be trusted. The desires of our hearts must be evaluated in light of the truth of God's word.

When it comes to your desires, the world will tell you to follow your heart. The problem is that the desires of your heart often don't line up with the desires of the Spirit. Here is how the Scriptures describe the condition of the human heart: "The human heart is the most deceitful of all things, and desperately wicked. Who really knows how bad it is? But I, the Lord, search all hearts and examine secret motives" (Jeremiah 17:9-10 NLT).

Therefore, you need to test your desires. Test them against the Scriptures. Test them by asking God to examine your motives. Test them by getting godly counsel. If you are going to follow the promptings of the Spirit, you need discernment, wisdom, and a commitment to God's revealed written Word.

But don't let those prerequisites prevent you from following the Holy Spirit's genuine prompting. The more you learn how to discern the promptings of the Spirit and follow them, the more you will experience the Spirit-filled life. Spirit-filled people also listen to and take advice from others.

The Holy Spirit Speaks Through Others

A friend of mine said it is amazing how often the voice of the Holy Spirit sounds like the voice of his wife. That is because God often uses others, especially those who are close to you, to speak to you. That doesn't mean that every piece of advice your friends and family give you is Spirit-breathed. You always need to test what you hear from others to determine if God is speaking to you through them. Still, the Holy Spirit will use other people to speak to you at times in your life.

The Scriptures tell us that in order to gain wisdom, we must get godly counsel from others. "Plans go wrong for lack of advice; many advisers bring success" (Proverbs 15:22 NLT). There is wisdom in seeking counsel from godly people.

That is why the local church is so important. As a Christ follower, you are part of the body of Christ. You are connected to many others. You need the other members as much as they need you.

"Yes, there are many parts, but only one body. The eye can never say to the hand, 'I don't need you.' The head can't say to the feet, 'I don't need you' (1 Corinthians 12:20-21 NLT).

Every person in the church is needed for spiritual growth and development to occur. We need to do our part and speak words of truth and grace, with love, into each other's lives. A small group, a class, or a mentoring relationship can provide opportunities for God to speak to you through others. You need to regularly and intentionally place yourself in structured environments in which there are small groups of people with whom you can have authentic relationships. It is in these small group environments that you can forge relationships with people who will counsel, admonish, and encourage you. These trusted people in your life should be a primary source from which you get wisdom and hear the Spirit speaking to you.

That is one reason the Apostle Paul instructed the churches he planted to each elect a group of elders. The churches needed the wisdom that came from groups of godly people working together. The church wasn't created to be run by a dictator or controlled by one person. God speaks to and guides the church through groups of godly people.

When I was around the age of 21, I felt God's call on my life to work for the local church in a full-time capacity. I went to seminary for my Master of Divinity degree. While in school, I took a part-time job at a local church as an associate pastor, but as time went on and things got tougher, I got discouraged. I didn't finish my degree, and I left my part-time position at the church.

I took a full-time job working in the business world. Later I got married and had kids, but God's call never left. 17 years later I was sitting at my desk at work when God began to stir my heart again to work in full-time ministry. I was working for a great company at the time, in which I had a promising future. But I was discontent. I felt God was calling me to make the transition from a career in information technology to vocational ministry within the local church. I experienced a holy discontentment.

That is often how God calls. You will experience an inward call or holy discontentment about your current circumstances and feel inner promptings from the Spirit. And if God is really speaking to you and calling you out, you will experience an outward call, too. The outward call is confirmation by others about what God has been speaking to you inwardly. That is how God has confirmed his call to many people throughout the ages. There is wisdom in godly counsel; the Holy Spirit uses others to speak to us.

My outward call and confirmation began with my wife. I spoke to her about what I sensed God was prompting me to do. She confirmed what I had been feeling. I went to a pastor at my church to get his feedback. He also agreed. I spent the next year consecrating my life to God in preparation for whatever he was going to do with me. After the year had passed, I was invited to interview for the position of children's pastor at West Ridge Church.

Some of the staff interviewed me. The elders met with me. They all agreed with what I had been feeling. God was calling me to be a pastor. That was 10 years ago. I still work full-time at West Ridge Church. I have experienced the joy of fulfilling God's call on my life as I have listened to the inner promptings of the Spirit and to the voices of other godly people. God speaks to us through others.

The problem is, many refuse to listen. Some don't listen because they are too busy. Others don't listen because they are fearful. Still others ignore the tug of inner promptings and the warnings and advice of others. They don't listen to God. Rather, they choose to go their own way and do their own thing. All of them miss out on the excitement of living the Spirit-filled life.

God wants you to experience the Spirit-filled life and fulfill your purpose here on earth. He wants a life filled with adventure for you, a life filled with power, a life characterized by peace. When you listen to the Spirit speak to you through others, you allow God to work in your life to help you get to that place. God also uses circumstances to speak to you. That happened to me in an unforgettable way when I was a teenager.

The Holy Spirit Speaks Through Circumstances

I was playing guitar for a cover band in the late 1980s. One evening, while practicing a new song at home in my bedroom, my guitar shorted out. Instead of hearing my guitar through my amp, I heard a preacher from a local radio show. The metal strings on my electric guitar served as an antenna and transmitted the radio signal of a gospel channel. I was transported from a concert hall to a sanctuary.

The preacher was speaking about the dangers of knowing the truth and turning away from it. I felt like that message was aimed directly at me. It was the exact struggle I had been experiencing. I hadn't been listening to the promptings of the Spirit. I'd kept turning away. I knew I needed to turn back to God.

As soon as the preacher finished his message, my guitar lost contact with the radio station. I sat there in a daze. I couldn't believe what had just happened. It seemed surreal.

God got my attention that night. The Holy Spirit spoke to me through some unusual circumstances, and I made some life-changing decisions because of it. God orchestrated the technical problems with my guitar, and the decisions I made as a result ended up changing my life's trajectory.

God controls all of the circumstances surrounding your life, too. Everything that comes your way must pass through his sovereign hands. The Holy Spirit uses those circumstances to speak to you. That happened time after time to people in the Scriptures, sometimes in unusual ways. God used a donkey to speak to Balaam. He used a burning bush to speak to Moses. He sent a whale to swallow Jonah. He blinded Paul with a light from heaven.

There are many examples in the Bible of God using circumstances, sometimes unusual ones, to speak to people. No two experiences are exactly alike. The circumstances the Holy Spirit uses to speak to you will be unique, too.

The Providence of God

God is continually involved in all of the circumstances of your life. All created things are held together by his power. God has an ongoing relationship with his creation. He didn't create the world, take a step back, and let it take its own course. He is constantly at work in our lives and in our world. This theological concept is called the providence of God.

The providence of God rules out chance, luck, and coincidences in your life. The Scriptures tell us that even the random scattering of objects are under God's control. "The lot is cast into the lap, but its every decision is from the Lord" (Proverbs 16:33 NLT). An interruption is a divine appointment. A coincidence is God's fingerprint. These things are reminders of his love, care, and control in your life. He doesn't watch your life from afar, occasionally taking a glance your way. He is closely and personally engaged in every circumstance.

As I work closely with families who have lost loved ones, I have observed a pattern in how God uses circumstances to help comfort grieving families. Often God will send what a friend of mine calls "kisses from heaven."

For example, one friend's dad always gave him dimes. After he died, dimes would appear in surprising places. They were "kisses from heaven," or God controlling circumstances to speak to his grieving child and bring him comfort.

My wife's dad loved yellow finches. After he passed away, especially when my wife was missing her dad, a yellow finch would show up outside our window. They were her "kisses from heaven."

I have heard similar stories over and over from other families. God controls the circumstances of your life to remind you that he cares. The truth is that God is more closely involved with your life than you probably realize. The Apostle Paul said, "For in him we live and move and exist" (Acts 17:28a NLT).

He knows when you get up and when you go to bed. He knows all your thoughts. He knows when you are late for work. He knows when you are stuck in traffic. David said to God, "You know when I sit down or stand up. You know my thoughts even when I'm far away. You see me when I travel and when I rest at home. You know everything I do" (Psalm 139:2-3 NLT).

God has incredible knowledge concerning every detail of your life. There is nowhere you can go where the Holy Spirit is not. The Psalmist said, "I can never escape from your Spirit! I can never get away from your presence! If I go up to heaven, you are there; if I go down to the grave, you are there. If I ride the wings of the morning, if I dwell by the farthest oceans, even there your hand will guide me, and your strength will support me" (Psalm 139:7-10 NLT).

Not only does he have comprehensive knowledge concerning the details of your life, but he also ordained your days before you were born. The Psalmist said, "You saw me before I was born. Every day of my life was recorded in your book. Every moment was laid out before a single day had passed" (Psalm 139:16 NLT). Your days, your steps, your movements, your heart, and your abilities are all under the providential care of God.

This doesn't nullify your responsibility for your daily decisions and actions. You are accountable for the things you say and do. The Scriptures don't easily reconcile the tension that exists between God's sovereignty and human responsibility. It is difficult to understand how they can coexist, but they are both true principles that the Scriptures affirm.

The comprehension of how it all works together is left for God to understand. You can find hope in knowing that he is in control and intimately involved behind the scenes of your life. Knowing that he has the power to bring about his purposes and plans for your life also gives you confidence.

You need to look at the events of your life through the eyes of faith. The Holy Spirit wants to speak to you through them. His voice might come via a closed door or an open door, a blessing or a challenge, a good experience or a bad experience.

Whatever the circumstance may be, ask God, "Is there something I need to see, learn, or do from this?" Look for ways that God is involved in the events of your daily life. Look for where he is working. Thank Him, trust Him, and talk to him about it. Pray for wisdom. Pray for circumstances to change. Pray for his peace in the midst of the difficult times. Most importantly, take comfort in knowing that he is providentially directing and caring for you through the journey of life.

Part 4
EXPERIENCING PEACE

Chapter 15
PEACE WITH GOD

Until Jesus returns, our enemy is vanquished, our bodies are made new, and the world is restored, we will continue to experience trials and sorrows in this world.

Yet, in the midst of trouble, you can have peace, peace that gives you strength, calms your fears, and offers you hope, peace that only Jesus can give.

Jesus said, "I am leaving you with a gift—peace of mind and heart. And the peace I give is a gift the world cannot give. So don't be troubled or afraid" (John 14:27 NLT).

Peace in our personal lives begins with a person, Jesus.

Jesus said, "I am the way, the truth, and the life. No one can come to the Father except through me" (John 14:6 NLT).

There is only way one to God. It isn't through Buddha, Muhammad, or any other person. The only way to God is through Jesus. This is an exclusive message in an inclusive world.

When you believe Jesus is who he said he is and trust in him for the forgiveness of your sins, only then can you have *peace with*

God. The Apostle Paul wrote, "Therefore, since we have been made right in God's sight by faith, we have peace with God because of what Jesus Christ our Lord has done for us" (Romans 5:1 NLT). Jesus makes it possible for you to experience peace in every area of your life.

Peace Through Justification

We lack peace because we have turned our backs on God and gone our own way. We have rebelled and sinned, desiring to live a life independent of God. The truth is, we all fall short in some aspect of our lives, no matter how good we think we are. The Scriptures tell us, "For everyone has sinned; we all fall short of God's glorious standard" (Romans 3:23 NLT).

If we stand before God to give an account of our lives based on our own merits, we will be declared guilty. We alone will bear the consequences for our sin without the help of Jesus. We will receive just punishment.

The good news is that Jesus paid the penalty for your sin once and for all when he died on the cross. You are no longer excluded because of your rebellion. You are no longer condemned for your sins. "So now there is no condemnation for those who belong to Christ Jesus" (Romans 8:1 NLT).

In Jesus, your past, present, and future sins are forgiven. You can make peace with your past because all of your sins have been cast as far as the east is from the west, thrown into the depths of the sea and remembered no more.

When you place your faith in Christ, your legal standing before God changes from "guilty" to "forgiven." It is a forensic act, decreed by the Most High Judge in the highest court. Justification is a one-time act based solely on the grace of God. The Scriptures tell us that we are justified by grace through faith.

"God saved you by his grace when you believed. And you can't take credit for this; it is a gift from God. Salvation is not a reward for the good things we have done, so none of us can boast about it" (Ephesians 2:8-9 NLT).

You can't take credit for your salvation. You can't earn it. You can't claim it as your birthright. It is a gift.

This teaching found in the Scriptures stands in contrast to the prevailing worldview that says acceptance into heaven is based on your own merits. You don't get into heaven by doing more good than bad. God's standard doesn't work that way. His standard is holiness. It requires perfection, and none of us are perfect.

You receive salvation by grace through faith. It happens at the heart level. "For it is by believing in your heart that you are made right with God, and it is by openly declaring your faith that you are saved" (Romans 10:10 NLT).

The experience of salvation is a work of God in your life that saves you from this world that is passing away. It also guarantees you safe passage to your home in a new world that will never pass away. It is a promise of eternal life. You have been saved from your past, you are being saved in the present, and you will be saved completely in the future.

Being saved means you are pardoned from eternal punishment, the consequence of your sin, and receive the righteousness of Christ. You give your sin to Jesus, and he gives you his righteousness in return. It is a great exchange. Adam's sin was given to you by birth, but Jesus' righteousness is given to you by faith.

While there is peace in knowing that you have been saved from the power and guilt of sin, there is also peace in knowing that your eternal destination has been forever changed. God assures you that you will have eternal life.

"For God loved the world so much that he gave his one and only Son, so that everyone who believes in him will not perish but have eternal life" (John 3:16 NLT).

If you believe, you will receive. It is a promise.

Peace in Assurance of Your Salvation

As a pastor I am often asked if I think people can lose their salvation. Is there anything you can do, or not do, that would cause you to lose eternal life once it has been given to you? Based on the promises of God, the quick answer is "No!" God doesn't give the gift of eternal life and then take it away.

This concept has been explained definitely by theologians throughout the ages in a doctrine called "the perseverance of the saints." This doctrine says that "all those who are truly born again will be kept by God's power and will persevere as Christians until the end of their lives, and that only those who persevere until the end have been truly born again."[19]

If you are truly born again and have received eternal life, you have assurance of your salvation. Your salvation is dependent on God's power and not your own. You have this promise from Jesus: "I give them eternal life, and they will never perish. No one can snatch them away from me, for my Father has given them to me, and he is more powerful than anyone else. No one can snatch them from the Father's hand. The Father and I are one" (John 10:28-30 NLT).

The Apostle Paul had complete confidence in God's ability to complete the work he starts in us at the moment of salvation. He said, "And I am certain that God, who began the good work within you, will continue his work until it is finally finished on the day when Christ Jesus returns" (Philippians 1:6 NLT).

Salvation is a work started by God, maintained by God, and completed by God. You can have peace and assurance because he is in control of your salvation.

But you also have to work out your salvation. You have a part to play. You can't sit back and do nothing. People who are truly saved persevere. Jesus said to the people who believed in him, "You are truly my disciples if you remain faithful to my teachings" (John 8:31 NLT).

If you have been born again, you will continue to persevere until the end. It doesn't mean you won't falter and fail along the way. You will. But you will persevere because of God's power working through you.

Those who abandon their faith show that they really never had faith to begin with. The Apostle John shared about people like this in the early church. "These people left our churches, but they never really belonged with us; otherwise they would have stayed with us. When they left, it proved that they did not belong with us" (I John 2:19 NLT).

Another way the Spirit gives you peace after you place your trust in Christ for salvation is by assuring you that you are a child of God.

Peace Comes from Being a Child of God

Many of us have been hurt by things our parents did or didn't do. When you become a child of God, the peace of our perfect

Heavenly Father can heal the hurt and disappointment you may have experienced at the hands of your earthly parents.

The truth is that many of us were wounded by the words of a mom or dad growing up. One woman said, "My step dad once said, 'Nobody cares how you feel.' I was about 8 I guess - he was driving and I was sitting in the backseat. I remember his voice and the tone, and it cut me to the quick. I remember keeping my face turned to the window so my stepsister wouldn't see me cry. It was just a terrible thing to say and I will never forget it."[20]

Parents can say many hurtful things. "I wish you'd have never been born." "You'll never amount to anything." "Nobody cares how you feel." "You are such a mama's boy." "You are the reason my marriage didn't work out." "You are worthless." "I hate you."

Words like these stick with you for life. The old adage, "sticks and stones may break my bones, but words will never hurt me" may help children ignore taunts from friends on the playground, but unfortunately it won't remove the sting from hurtful words spoken by a parent. Words have great power, and the wrong words can hurt us deeply. The Scriptures tell us, "Death and life are in the power of the tongue" (Proverbs 18:21a NLT). The words we hear as children impact us throughout life.

Some of your wounds may have come from words, but others may have come from a parent's absence in your life. Perhaps your father or mother wasn't there for you. Maybe he walked out on your family. Maybe she never attended any of your events as a child. Maybe he didn't give you words of encouragement. Maybe she was apathetic. Maybe he was caught up in his hobbies or addictions. Maybe she passed away and couldn't be there for you. Whatever the circumstance, your parents' absence in your life left wounds.

In some instances, the wounds may be physical. They abused you. They were angry and took their frustration out on you. They hit you. They took corporal punishment to the extreme. Or maybe they abused you sexually. Those are difficult wounds to overcome.

The truth is, all of our parents fell short just as Adam and Eve did. They are sinners just like us. Some sins were greater and did more damage; some were less egregious but still hurt.

The fact that your parents are sinners doesn't excuse any of the wrongs they did to you, but it is does explain why they did what they did. Unlike our Heavenly Father, no earthly parent is perfect. This doesn't mean that all parents are bad, but it does mean they all fall short in some way. As a result, many of us have parent wounds.

I have my own parent wounds, and my mom and dad have theirs. All of us can trace these wounds back to our first parents, Adam and Eve. The cycle of hurt has been perpetuated ever since our first parents sinned and fell from grace.

I am guilty, too. I have wounded my kids, exploding in anger or yelling at times when words of tenderness were needed. I apologize whenever I hurt them with my words because I know how deep those wounds go and how long they stick with you. I make an effort to regulate my words because I know they have power to heal and to hurt.

Many of the problems we face can be traced back to issues with our earthly parents. Your experiences in childhood affect how you view the world and others. They affect your romantic relationships and the way you interact with authority figures. Your relationship with your parents has a long-lasting impact on your life.

The hope of the gospel is that your parent wounds will begin to heal when you become a child of our perfect Heavenly Father. "But to all who believed him and accepted him, he gave the right to become children of God" (John 1:12 NLT).

Where your earthly parents fell short, your Heavenly Father never will. He is perfect, and you can experience his perfect love. No matter how messed up and dysfunctional your parents were, you can be assured that your Father in Heaven is perfect in every way.

The Holy Spirit gives us assurance that we are God's children in the depths of our being. "For his Spirit joins with our spirit to affirm that we are God's children" (Romans 8:16 NLT). Your relationship with your Father in Heaven can become closer and dearer than any other relationship you have on earth. That is God's desire for you.

As God's child you have been adopted into his royal family. The Apostle Paul wrote, "You received God's Spirit when he adopted you as his own children. Now we call him, "Abba, Father" (Romans 8:15 NLT).

You never have to worry about being abandoned by your Heavenly Father. He will never leave you or forsake you. You never have to worry that your Heavenly Father might wound you with his words. He will only speak words of life to you. The Spirit will reassure you, comfort you, and remind you of the promises your Heavenly Father has for you.

As his child, you have a great inheritance in the coming Kingdom, an inheritance involving eternal riches. The Apostle Peter said, "and we have a priceless inheritance—an inheritance that is kept in heaven for you, pure and undefiled, beyond the reach of change and decay" (I Peter 1:4 NLT).

The riches of this world will pass away, but the riches of heaven will last forever. You may not have much in this world, but as God's adopted child, you will have more than you could hope for or imagine in the Kingdom.

While the ultimate fulfillment of your inheritance in God's Kingdom will be found in heaven and the new earth, you can experience aspects of the Kingdom here and now. You can experience the peace that comes from having the Kingdom of God in your heart, the peace *of* God.

Chapter 16

PEACE OF GOD

I was eating lunch with my mother one day when she stopped in the middle of our meal and said, "I need to tell you something." I had a feeling that the "something" she needed to tell me wasn't good. It wasn't.

She said, "My doctor discovered some lumps in my colon that he is concerned about." I told her, "I'm sure it's nothing to worry about." I wanted to reassure her everything was going to be OK, but I could tell from the look in her eyes that she was concerned.

I was concerned, too. Still, I hoped to hear good news after her follow-up visit with her doctor. I knew that my mother wasn't a smoker or a drinker. She had always been in perfect health.

My mom went to her doctor for the follow-up visit, and he confirmed her worst fears. It was cancer. My aunt called my wife while I was at work to tell her the news. I don't think my mom wanted to be the one to break it to me.

I didn't get home until late that night. My wife was waiting up for me, and I knew something was wrong. She said she didn't know how to tell me, but the doctors had confirmed that my mom had ovarian cancer, and they needed to do surgery immediately. This was serious. I remember the shock I experienced in that moment. This couldn't be happening. Cancer was something that affected other people, not us.

My mom had surgery the next week to remove the cancerous tumors from her body. On that day, I sat prayerfully and quietly in the waiting room. After the surgery, the doctor came out and asked us to come into a small room for a debriefing. At that point, I didn't know whether she had lived or died during the operation. The doctor had a look of concern on his face.

He looked at us and said she had done well. I exhaled a sigh of relief. Then he told us the bad news.

The cancer had spread much further than he had first thought. It was in an advanced stage. He had removed a tumor the size of a grapefruit as well as several smaller ones from the surrounding area. He explained that he had also had to remove a large part of her colon due to the cancer's spread in her abdomen. There were cancerous spots remaining on her liver and pancreas that he had been unable to surgically remove.

The doctor told us it was critical that my mother start chemotherapy as soon as possible. Again I thought to myself, 'this can't be happening to my family.'

Bad news has a way of feeling surreal. When we get bad news that alters our view of the future, we shield ourselves through denial. It helps cushion the shock of reality. I was numb.

I am an only child. At that moment, I wanted a brother or sister with whom I could share my emotions. Instead, I dealt with my pain inwardly. I experienced depression and anger about the situation.

Throughout the succeeding days, I even sought to escape reality in unhealthy ways but my efforts didn't take make the situation less real.

There are a lot of unhealthy rhythms you can fall into while living in a chaotic world. In an effort to escape, you may abuse alcohol or other drugs. They numb the pain, but only temporarily. You may hide yourself in your work. You may seek sinful pleasures that provide temporary relief.

None of these things will make the situation go away. In fact, they will make things worse, robbing you of the peace you so desperately need. Be aware of unhealthy coping mechanisms that you may develop during difficult times.

My mom didn't try to escape from the reality of the news. She chose to face it head on, to fight. She was determined to give all she had to overcome this terrible disease.

After surgery, she endured the discomfort of chemotherapy. I don't think she ever complained during the 10 plus chemo treatments she experienced over the next two years.

Unfortunately, the form of cancer she had was very aggressive. Occasionally it would respond to chemo, but not for long. After a couple of years of persistent treatments, the cancer was no longer responding at all. It was growing. It got to the point that my mother could no longer keep food down because of the tumors in her stomach. She was given a feeding tube for nourishment. The doctors also had to insert a tube into her stomach to drain fluids into an external bag she kept around her waist.

My mother with my oldest daughter, Haley.

After several months, the doctors met with my mom to discuss options. They presented her with a tough decision. If she continued to use the feeding tubes, cancerous tumors would start to break through her skin. The doctors didn't advise that option. The other choice was to remove the feeding tubes and let the cancer take its natural course. She would starve to death in the process.

The decision was hers to make. Neither option was good, but there were no others. She had tried everything, and there would be no cure.

She decided to remove the tubes. She told me she was at peace with her decision. She was at *peace with God*, but she was also experiencing the *peace of God* in her decision. She knew that she would die soon, and yet the peace of God comforted her. I watched that peace surround her heart and mind.

The peace of God is a supernatural strength that helps us in the midst of adversity. It guards your heart and mind. The Scriptures tell us, "His peace will guard your hearts and minds as you live in Christ Jesus" (Philippians 4:7 NLT). My mom experienced the peace of God in her final days.

We scheduled home hospice care for her after she made her decision. She didn't live very long after that. At the age of 57, she breathed her last breath lying on the couch in her home. After she died, I looked at her lifeless body and grieved over the things our family had lost that day. I wouldn't see my mom grow old. My two daughters would no longer have a "Nana." There would be no more long talks or motherly advice. I would greatly miss her presence in my life. I wept.

In one sense, I was glad for her. I knew her suffering was over. I knew she was home. She was completely healed and happy in a real place called heaven. But I was so sad for myself and the rest of us who were left behind.

God gave my mom peace in her last days, and he gave me peace in the days and months after her death. I still hurt. I still missed her. But I had the peace of God guarding my heart and mind. This is the peace Jesus promised: "I am leaving you with a gift—peace of mind and heart. And the peace I give is a gift the world cannot give. So don't be troubled or afraid" (John 14:27 NLT).

The peace of God is a gift from God. I've received this peace that defies explanation, and I've seen my mom and others receive it.

Some of the others I have witnessed experience God's peace in the midst of trouble are children with cancer. Our family has served multiple times with an organization called Blue Skies. Blue Skies provides week-long retreats at the beach for families facing pediatric cancer. Children who have cancer face long hospital visits and receive ongoing treatment that causes them pain, sickness, and hair loss. Some face terminal cases, but they seem to have an extra dose of God's peace guarding their hearts and minds. They are often happy and try to cheer others up, more concerned about others' feelings than their own. The peace of God is working in their lives.

You can experience that same peace. The peace of God will help you when you face hardship. All you need to do is talk to God about what is weighing you down and trust him to give you strength to face whatever lies ahead.

Peace Through Prayer

One of the ways you can access this heavenly peace is through prayer. Worry, fear, and anxiety break in and rob you of peace. Prayer locks the doors and guards the house. The peace of God protects you from the robbers of peace.

Prayer is simple, but it is often one of the spiritual disciplines we struggle with the most. The benefits of prayer, however, make it worth doing. Prayer has the ability to change both you and your circumstances.

Prayer changes you. When you pray your desires are sifted. Your heart is connected to your Creator's. You experience a deeper fellowship with God. You exchange your anxious thoughts for God's peace. That's a good trade!

Not only do your prayers change you, but they also change your circumstances. Some people feel that prayer is a waste of time. They rationalize that God will do what he wants to do whether they pray or not. They wonder if their prayers really make a difference. But the Scriptures teach us that our prayers do make a difference. They have an impact on us and the world around us.

James, the brother of Jesus wrote, "The earnest prayer of a righteous person has great power and produces wonderful results" (James 5:16b NLT).

You may read that verse and feel that you are not a super spiritual person. You doubt that your prayers are as powerful as the prayers offered by pastors or the people you read about in the Bible. James answers these questions. He says, "Elijah was as human as we are, and yet when he prayed earnestly that no rain would fall, none fell for three and a half years!" (James 5:17 NLT).

James reminds us that Elijah was human. He was an ordinary man, just like you and me, who prayed and believed, and his prayers changed the circumstances around him in a powerful way. He prayed that it wouldn't rain, and it didn't! That should give you encouragement to pray about your personal situations and the circumstances that affect your life. You prayers do make a difference!

When you pray, you invite God to get involved in your situation. Prayer is an expression of your dependence on him and a declaration of your faith. When you pray, you are saying, "God I need you!" and "I need you to change these circumstances!" You have an active role to play in our world by praying. God wants you to join him in changing the events and circumstances surrounding you each day.

Jesus explained what effective prayer looks like. He said you should, "Keep on asking, and you will receive what you ask for. Keep on seeking, and you will find. Keep on knocking, and the door will be opened to you. For everyone who asks, receives. Everyone who seeks, finds. And to everyone who knocks, the door will be opened" (Matthew 7:7-8 NLT).

When you ask, seek, and knock, doors will be opened for you. That is a promise! There is a clear connection between seeking and receiving. That is why Jesus said *keep on* asking, seeking, and knocking. Don't give up until you get an answer!

The most difficult circumstances you face must be met with prayer. Prayer can change those circumstances, making things that seem impossible possible, things that seem immovable movable, and things that seem inaccessible accessible.

Karl Barth wrote, "To clasp the hands in prayer is the beginning of an uprising against the disorder of the world."[21] Your prayers have the power to move the heart of God to act and change the circumstances in an out-of-control world. Be a part of the uprising and change your world through prayer!

Chapter 17
PEACE WITH OTHERS

When you have peace with God and the peace of God, it is much easier to have peace with others. Having peace with others doesn't mean you will never experience conflict or opposition. Jesus experienced both, and you will, too. But you should strive to live at peace with others as much as it is possible. The Scriptures say, "Do all that you can to live in peace with everyone" (Romans 12:18 NLT).

Loving Others

In order to live at peace with others, you have to grow in your love for God and people. This is the supreme distinctive of life in the Kingdom of God. It is what makes us a peculiar people in a broken world. It should set us apart. Jesus said, "Your love for one another will prove to the world that you are my disciples" (John 13:35-36 NLT).

The world should know us by our love first, not by our condemnation or opposition.

Jesus said the most important thing you can do in life is love. "'You must love the Lord your God with all your heart, all your soul, and all your mind. This is the first and greatest commandment. A second is equally important: 'Love your neighbor as yourself.' The entire law and all the demands of the prophets are based on these two commandments" (Matthew 22:37-40 NLT).

You were created to love God and love people more than anything else in life. When Adam and Eve sinned in the beginning, it marred God's image in us. Our sinful natures caused us to become self-absorbed, to wrongly put ourselves first. When you love God first and others second, however, you will function the way you were created to. Love gets your eyes off of yourself and back on God and others where they belong.

There is an old parable that describes the difference between people who love and people who don't. In this parable there are two sets of people, those in heaven and those in hell. Both sets of people sit at a table to dine and are given plenty of food to eat, but their spoons are so long that the people are unable to feed themselves. They have to figure out how to eat.

In hell, the people are starving because they can't hold the spoons and feed themselves at the same time. In heaven, the people are well fed because they feed one another across the table. The people in heaven love one another, and their love leads them to look to each other's needs first. As they do, everyone's needs are met. Love is like that. There is peace and harmony when we love one another the way God intended.

Love is the essence of God's nature, and since he is eternal, his love is eternal. He has a limitless supply of love to pour out on each of us. The Scriptures repeat over and over that "his faithful love endures forever" (Psalm 136:1b NLT). The well of his love will never run dry. When you love God with all of your heart, he fills your love tank in return.

The love of God will loosen the grip of other things that try to control you. Love conquers all. Love breaks down barriers. It doesn't just happen accidentally either. You have to choose to love, yielding to God's will. No one can force love upon you. You must choose it for yourself.

Choosing love might be harder for some people because of their pasts. Some people grew up in homes where love was not present. They were neglected or abused as children. But there is still hope. If you grew up in a situation devoid of much love, you can still be a loving person. It may be more difficult for you than it is for others, but it isn't impossible. Love can be learned, and all things are possible with God.

For example, the Apostle Paul was filled with hatred before his conversion. He persecuted Christians and ordered them to be killed, but God transformed his life. Paul would go on to give his life for the sake of others and write some of the most well-known passages in the Scriptures about what it means to love.

Whatever your background, becoming a loving person should be one of your greatest aspirations. You won't go wrong in life by making it your number one priority to love God and people. Love won't magically fix all your relationships, making them problem-free. But it will lift the burden of control off of you. Love lifts the burden of trying to manage other people's emotions and behaviors. It allows you to give to others and realize that you are only responsible for your actions and not how others respond.

The Apostle Paul learned how important this was to his life. He said if he could speak all the languages of the earth and heaven and didn't love others, he would have gained nothing. If he had the ability to predict the future and understand all the mysteries of God and life and didn't love others, he would have gained nothing. If he gave everything he had to help the poor and didn't love others, he would have gained nothing.

He said love should be our greatest pursuit and defined it this way:

> Love is patient and kind.
> Love is not jealous or boastful or proud or rude.
> It does not demand its own way.
> It is not irritable, and it keeps no record of being
> wronged.
> It does not rejoice about injustice but rejoices
> whenever the truth wins out.
> Love never gives up, never loses faith, is always
> hopeful, and endures through every
> circumstance (1 Corinthians 13:4-7 NLT).

For love to be patient and kind, it must be respectful of differences. It must listen and seek to understand, taking care not to misinterpret disagreement as hate. Disagreement and love are not mutually exclusive. You can love someone and disagree with them.

Love accepts others. When you accept people, you connect with all parts of them, good and bad, strong and weak, healthy and broken. You may not agree with everything they believe, but you accept the reality of who they are.[22]

Love validates others. Dr. John Townsend says, "We all need to have our experiences and our feelings validated by others. To validate is to attribute reality and seriousness to something or someone. Validation comes from the term valid, meaning 'grounded and meaningful.' So when someone validates your experiences, they are saying, in effect, 'What you are saying and feeling is real, and I'm taking it seriously, because I take you seriously.' They are, in effect, placing a 'validation stamp' on your feelings, in the same way that a judge validates a contract between two parties. As the agreement is now a binding reality, so your experience is a reality that makes a difference to the other person."[23]

Love also speaks the truth in love. It doesn't keep quiet about the truth, but it always speaks it with love and compassion. It goes to other people in humility, speaking out not to prove a point, but because it wants what is best for others.

Loving others would be easy if people were easy to love, wouldn't it? But often they aren't. Even those closest to us can be difficult to love at times. They have quirks. They hurt or disappoint us. You and I can be hard to love sometimes, too. We need to remember that we all fall short when it comes to love.

Love Forgives

That is why love requires forgiveness. Forgiveness is a willful decision to give up the desire to repay someone for the wrong he or she did to you. Forgiveness leaves vengeance in the hands of God, letting go and letting God deal with the person as he sees fit. Your job is not to repay; it is to forgive.

Forgiveness involves giving up negative thoughts and feelings you have about the person who hurt you. Your feelings may not be ready to forgive yet, but you must choose to forgive anyway, trusting that your feelings will come around later. Forgiveness is often a process. It can take time for your heart to catch up with your head.

When it comes to forgiving others, it is important to understand what forgiveness is not. Forgiveness doesn't excuse the wrong done to you, perpetuate injustice, or enable bad behavior. It is a willful decision to grant a pardon and release feelings of resentment. You can forgive someone and still maintain healthy boundaries in order to protect yourself.

If you want to experience peace with others, you must regularly embrace the act of forgiveness. In a broken world, hurt people hurt people. The Apostle Peter struggled with the limits of forgiveness. He wanted to know how many times he had to forgive people when they sinned against him.

He asked Jesus, "Lord, how often should I forgive someone who sins against me? Seven times?"

"No, not seven times," Jesus replied, "but seventy times seven!" (Matthew 18:21-22 NLT).

Jesus' answer indicated that forgiveness is perpetual. You must keep forgiving without keeping count of wrongs.

While there is no limit to the number of times you should forgive, you still need healthy boundaries. Forgiveness doesn't mean putting yourself in verbally or physically abusive situations. You can forgive and still put boundaries in place to protect yourself from abusive people. That is what loving people do.

Do not confuse loving with enabling. Dr. Townsend says, "Loving people don't put up with evil and foolishness. That is enabling and rescuing, and it never helps anyone. People who are truly loving will confront, limit, and quarantine people who consistently make wrong choices. So keep that distinction in mind: love seeks the best, but it does not enable bad behavior."[24]

While we don't want to enable bad behavior, we still need to forgive. Forgiveness usually isn't our first reaction when we are wronged. It's our tendency to respond by withdrawing, defending ourselves, or retaliating. This is a defense mechanism.

But if you don't forgive, your hurt will turn into bitterness. You must deal with it. Someone once said, "Bitterness is like drinking poison and then hoping it will kill your enemies." Bitterness hurts you more than it does anyone else. In an out-of-control world, you can't control whether or not others hurt you, but you can control your response.

Satan wants you to harbor bitterness. He wants to cause chaos in your relationships. He wants you to experience discord and disunity. He doesn't want your relationships to be reconciled. He wants your soul to be poisoned by bitterness that destroys your life from within.

The Abbates' Story

Steven and Maryanne Abbate understand what it means to forgive. They have been members of our church for more than 10 years. I came to know them better after a tragedy involving one of their sons, a tragedy that changed their family forever.

Their son, Luke, was a popular 15-year-old athlete at Harrison High School. He played lacrosse and football. In February 2006, he was riding home after lacrosse practice with another teenager. The teen was driving recklessly and crashed into an embankment.

Luke was seriously injured. He was life-flighted to Atlanta Medical Center and placed on life support. After some time, it was apparent that there was nothing else the doctors could do. On top of dealing with all their emotions, his parents had to make the difficult decision whether or not to donate his organs. They decided they would. Luke's heart, one lung, kidneys, liver and pancreas were given to others in need. Luke's legacy lived on through the people who received his organs.

Much later, the teenage driver whose reckless driving had taken Luke's life appeared in court. Luke's mother wrote about that day and the process of forgiving him. With her permission, I am sharing her journey of forgiveness.

"On a blustery January day, I watched a young man be handcuffed, led out of the courtroom to be taken to a juvenile facility. Eleven months prior, that handcuffed teen made a reckless choice in an automobile that claimed the life of my son. The ramifications of that split-second decision were magnanimous-life altering; forever changing the landscape of our lives. Strangely, my heart felt unsatisfied-unsettled. Yes, earthly justice had been served but the heartache didn't end. My soul acknowledged there would never be enough justice on this earth. I couldn't have what I desperately wanted back, my beloved son. Some circumstances can never be fully righted on this earth.

I hated what he did. I still do. His choice was reprehensible. I wanted to hate him too for the heartache he caused my family. He haphazardly careened into our lives, leaving the scattered pieces of our hearts broken and bloody. The collateral damage seemed beyond repair. Bitter anger had begun to take root in my heart, gripping it, choking it, shrinking its capacity to receive. I knew deep in my soul that the power of hate could literally destroy me, making me another casualty of this terrible tragedy.

I desperately cried, 'Jesus, save me. I am drowning in the pain of loss and hate. Please, help me, guide me, do it through me. I choose to forgive.' My feelings haven't automatically aligned with my decision; forgiveness has been an ongoing process. Slowly, I release the layers of pain, anger, injustice, and the deep sadness of my heart. I have an abiding assurance that Jesus will heal me and seek righteous justice on my behalf. Jesus can be trusted with this young man's life; He is both just and merciful.

My choice has changed my destiny; my heart is expanding and openly postured to receive all that God has for me and my life. I know freedom from the shackles of hate. Miraculously, I can genuinely pray for this young man's soul to find the beautiful saving grace of Jesus to carry the burden of his guilt and redeem the pain of his choice. Forgiveness is a miracle. It is the path that invites the goodness of God to redeem and reframe our pain.

It will always trump evil."

Luke's life and the story of the Abbate family inspired the movie *The 5th Quarter*. I hope their story inspires you that forgiveness is possible.

Forgiveness like this is possible because God first forgave us. That is what the cross was all about. Jesus' death on the cross was necessary in order to bring peace and control back into our world. It was on the cross, in the midst of mockery, pain, and suffering, that Jesus said an incredible thing to the people who had beat him, spit on him, and crucified him. He said in his final hours, "Father, forgive them, for they do not know what they are doing" (Luke 23:34 NLT).

Each of us will experience moments in which we'll need to respond as Jesus did. You can't muster that kind of love in yourself. It can only come from God. When you don't have the strength to forgive others, God will help you if you ask him.

What Do You Do When Someone Sins Against You?

If someone sins against you and you forgive them, what else should you do? Should you say anything? Should you do anything?

If it was a minor offense, you can resolve it privately by overlooking whatever was said or done. That is an easy way to make peace. "Sensible people control their temper; they earn respect by overlooking wrongs" (Prov. 19:11 NLT). Sensible people aren't overly sensitive. They earn respect from others by not overreacting to every offense.

Ken Sande says, "Overlooking an offense is a form of forgiveness, and involves a deliberate decision not to talk about it, dwell on it, or let it grow into pent-up bitterness or anger."[25] If the offense isn't hurting someone else, if the person isn't hurting themselves, and if it doesn't permanently damage the relationship, then you should try to overlook it.

If the offense cannot be overlooked, then Jesus explains what to do next in order to restore peace to the relationship. "If another believer sins against you, go privately and point out the offense. If the other person listens and confesses it, you have won that person back" (Matthew 18:15 NLT).

The first thing to notice is that Jesus was addressing people who believed in him. He said, "If another believer sins against you..." Matthew 18 addresses sin and conflict within the church, not outside it. The Apostle Paul said, "It isn't my responsibility to judge outsiders, but it certainly is your responsibility to judge those inside the church who are sinning" (I Corinthians 5:12 NLT).

So if another believer sins against you, you should go privately to that person and discuss the offense. You should do this out of respect for you, the other person, and most importantly Jesus' commands. Instead of going to other people to talk *about* the person, go directly *to* the person to talk things out. This practice helps prevent misunderstandings and rumors from spreading, keeping the conflict contained between the two of you.

This seems like a simple and straightforward concept, but it has been my experience that few people practice it. I have observed that many people won't go privately to individuals who have injured them. Instead, they hold on to offenses and put up walls. They avoid the people with whom they're in conflict so that they don't have to deal with them or the issue. They go to other people to vent, trying to get them on their side. When that happens, a lot of people who shouldn't be involved get brought into the drama and triangulation occurs.

Triangulation happens when two people fail to resolve a conflict privately. One of them brings a third person in to take sides. The third person has no business in the conflict and only exacerbates the problem, making the other person feel ganged up on.

For example, Cindy is offended that Joan didn't invite her to lunch with the rest of their friends. Cindy finds out on Facebook about the lunch date from which she was excluded. She is hurt. Cindy posts a passive aggressive post on Facebook saying, "I guess I know who my real friends are!" Her other friends comment asking what has happened. She explains indirectly without naming Joan. Now all her friends on Facebook know that Cindy isn't happy with someone, and most have figured out whom.

That is how triangulation works. Other people were brought into an issue that should only have been between Cindy and Joan. Cindy wanted to punish Joan by venting her hurt on Facebook. She was also looking for validation. Rather than triangulate as Cindy did, you should go directly to the people who offended you, never bringing in others to take sides. For one thing, the people who offended you might not even know they did anything wrong. They might have no idea that they hurt you. You might assume that they know what they did, but it is possible that they don't.

That is what happened with Joan. When she sent out the invite on Facebook she accidentally sent the request to a different Cindy. She wasn't intentionally excluding Cindy; it was a simple mistake. Cindy ended up embarrassing herself by bringing in other people. Now Cindy has hurt Joan. If Joan doesn't follow the teaching of Jesus and talk to Cindy privately about this issue, the cycle will continue and their relationship will be damaged.

We have all had experiences like this. I once walked by someone at church who had done a lot of volunteer work for me. I was in a hurry and didn't see him or speak to him. I was focused on where I had to be and what I had to do, and I just didn't notice him. The person was standing there talking to another friend of mine, and after I walked by, he told my friend that it was very inconsiderate of me not to acknowledge him after all he had done to help me.

I wouldn't have known that I offended this person, but thankfully, my friend called to tell me. If the guy I offended would have talked to me directly, we could have resolved the problem easily without involving other people. He would have learned that I hadn't seen him and that I hadn't been snubbing him. I called him to apologize, and we were able to work it out.

When you have been hurt, offended, or sinned against, the best thing to do is go privately and humbly to the person who offended you. But before you go to him or her, check your heart. You don't want to go in pride and arrogance or with the desire to win an argument. Instead, go in humility after prayerful examining yourself.

Jesus advised us to examine ourselves first before approaching others about their problems. "And why worry about a speck in your friend's eye when you have a log in your own? How can you think of saying to your friend, 'Let me help you get rid of that speck in your eye,' when you can't see past the log in your own eye? Hypocrite! First get rid of the log in your own eye; then you will see well enough to deal with the speck in your friend's eye" (Matthew 7:3-5 NLT).

Examine yourself. Pray. Ask God to show you the log in your eye first. I have found that the things that bother or me in others are often flaws or weaknesses I myself struggle with. It is possible that the same is true for you. Be honest about your own problems first. When you are, you gain a sense of humility and empathy. Examining your own heart takes your eyes off the other person's offense and helps you see him or her on equal ground.

Don't assume the worst either. Assume that the person didn't realize what he or she did, that he or she didn't intend to hurt you. Consider that he or she may be dealing with something difficult that you weren't aware of, a dog's death or bad news from a doctor or a layoff or just a bad day. When you go in humility, you take these possibilities into consideration.

Different Types of People

It is also wise to think about the person you are approaching. Think about the best way and time to approach him or her based on his or her character. There are different types of people, and each type requires a different approach when it comes to confrontation. Some people are wise, some foolish, some simple; others are scoffers.[26] People can fluctuate between each type, too, at different times in their lives.

First there are *wise people*. They are teachable, calm, gentle, and peaceable. They think before they speak and act. They are easy to approach and will listen when you confront them: "correct the wise, and they will love you" (Proverbs 9:8b NLT). They will listen well and keep the matter private between the two of you.

Next there are *scoffers*. Scoffers are the exact opposite of wise people. They are not teachable. They are emotional, easily agitated, and often belligerent. They are not easy to approach.

They mock and ridicule everyone else with no regard to their own condition. They stir up trouble wherever they go. They especially like to hide behind computers and post comments that stir up hate online. They are trolls. That is why it is usually best not to engage them in online conversations. It only fuels their desire to argue and heap abuse.

When you have to confront a scoffer face to face, first consider if it is worth the effort. "Whoever corrects a scoffer gets himself abuse, and he who reproves a wicked man incurs injury" (Proverbs 9:7 ESV). Give prayerful consideration before asking for a face-to-face meeting. If the person is someone of the opposite sex, make sure you take someone else with you. If you do decide to ask for a meeting, put extra thought into how to approach the person. Ask for wisdom from others. Remember, even Jesus didn't respond to scoffers at times in his life.

Then there are *fools*. Fools aren't as bad as scoffers, but they are still difficult to confront. Fools despise wisdom and instruction (Proverbs 1:7 NLT). They lack common sense. They are complacent.

They talk more than they listen. They always see themselves as being right. "Fools think their own way is right, but the wise listen to others" (Proverbs 12:15 NLT). You may want to ask them to repeat back to you what they heard you say.

They may also slander you after you finish talking. You may want to stress the importance of keeping your conversation confidential.

Lastly, there are *simpletons*. They are easily misled. They believe everything and lack common sense. They run head first into danger, even when others have warned them against it. They have trouble applying wisdom to their lives. They are typically easy to approach but may be sensitive and get emotional. Once you address an issue, they may turn around and do it again.

Once you have checked your motives and considered the type of person you are approaching, go privately to him or her and address the issue. Have a conversation. Your interaction should be a two-way street; you need to both talk and listen. Start with affirmation. Let the person know what you appreciate about him or her. Be honest and sincere. Then address the issue.

Be Assertive

As you address the issue, be assertive. Don't be aggressive and yell. Don't be passive and sulk. Clearly state what it was that hurt you. Try and avoid making statements that begin with "you." For example, don't begin by saying, "You are so mean," or "You are insensitive," or "You don't care about anyone." Accusatory statements like that will put the other person on the defensive.

Take ownership of your feelings by using "I" statements. Say something like, "I am not sure if you are aware, but when you walked by the other day and didn't acknowledge me, I was hurt," or "I felt unappreciated when you forgot my birthday." Using "I" statements helps prevent defensiveness and allows you to own your feelings.

Also avoid the words "always" and "never." Don't say, "You *always* nag," or "You *never* listen to me when I talk to you." Those are extreme statements. Be specific, and don't exaggerate.

Then listen. Be ready to take your share of the blame if needed. Don't put up walls. It is rare for conflict to be one-sided. Actively listen by repeating back what the other person says in your own words. Listen for both the person's words and the feelings behind them.

When forgiveness is needed, express it. When rebuke is needed, state it. Try your best to find common ground. Pray with each other if you can. In the end, realize that confrontation is a messy process. Sometimes it will go better than you expect, and sometimes it will go worse.

You don't know how the person you're confronting will respond. You can't control his or her attitude or expectations. There is no guarantee that issues will be resolved easily every time. Sometimes they won't. The other person may walk out offended. He or she may disagree with you or shift the blame. Jesus knew this. That is why he offered additional steps.

If the first conversation was unsuccessful because you couldn't agree or the person continues to behave in the same way, you might need to meet again. "But if you are unsuccessful, take one or two others with you and go back again, so that everything you say may be confirmed by two or three witnesses" (Matthew 18:16 NLT).

If you need to ask for another meeting, take one or two other people with you. The other people you invite don't have to be witnesses to whatever the original offense was, but rather witnesses to the interaction between the two of you. Since Jesus was addressing how conflict should be handled in the church, this could involve asking a ministry leader, elder, or pastor to join you in the conversation. Such a person can help resolve the dispute and provide objective insight and wisdom. Depending on the type of person you are dealing with, he or she may not want to have another conversation and will turn down any other offers to meet. That is his or her decision. You can't force a person to have a conversation he or she doesn't want to have. That is why in some situations, after much time and prayer, you may need to move on to the next step.

"If the person still refuses to listen, take your case to the church" (Matthew 18:17a NLT). Each local church is different in how they want to handle these situations. Be sure to go through the proper channels at your church.

"If he or she won't accept the church's decision, treat that person as a pagan or a corrupt tax collector" (Matthew 18:17b NLT). In some situations, the elders or leadership team may have to ask a person, because of his or her unwillingness to abide by the decision of the church, to leave their fellowship.

I have seen this done in rare situations. Whenever I have, it has taken much time, counsel, and prayer by the leaders of the church. It is done in love and not in vengeance. When it is done well, I have seen reconciliation happen at a later time. I have seen marriages saved because of these steps. I have seen people humbled by their church's tough love come back later to apologize. The ultimate objective Jesus wants is restoration. He desires that people be reconciled and restored to himself and to one another.

The reality, however, is that not all relationships can be restored in a broken world. Some people won't come back. Some leave and never return. Some don't want to be restored. Satan will never be an angel again. Judas will never be a disciple again. You have to trust that God will take care of those people in his way and in his time.

There also may be times at which it is not safe or physically possible to approach a person face to face. Maybe the person is abusive or lives somewhere you can't reach. Maybe he or she has passed away.

When you can't speak face to face with a person, it can be therapeutic to have a conversation with him or her as if he or she were actually there. Set up an empty chair and talk to the person. If that seems awkward, write a letter to him or her. Acknowledge your hurt. Acknowledge the anger you may be feeling. Forgive. Doing this could help bring you peace when a face-to-face conversation isn't possible.

Jesus Came to Bring a Sword, not Peace

In the midst of talking about peace, we find that Jesus said something startling. He said, "Don't imagine that I came to bring peace to the earth! I came not to bring peace, but a sword" (Matthew 10:34 NLT).

Why would he say that?

To be clear, he wasn't asking his followers to take up swords and kill unbelievers or overthrow the government. He was letting us know that when a person pledges allegiance to him, it can cause conflict within his or her family. It could even cause family members to become enemies.

Jesus said, "If you love your father or mother more than you love me, you are not worthy of being mine; or if you love your son or daughter more than me, you are not worthy of being mine" (Matthew 10:37 NLT).

Your love for Jesus should take precedence over your love for all other people, including the people in your very own family. He asks you to love him more than you love your parents, your spouse, and your children. He wants to be your first love.

Peace in Our Families

Sometimes the most difficult place to find peace is within our families. There can be friction and argumentation between husbands and wives parents and kids, brothers and sisters. That is what happens when sinful people live under the same roof. Conflict is normal, but it can rob you of peace if it isn't resolved. The Scriptures explain the ideal dynamics between family members.

For wives they say: "Submit to your husbands as to the Lord" (Galatians 5:22 NLT).

For husbands they say: "Love your wives, just as Christ loved the church. He gave up his life for her" (Galatians 5:25 NLT).

For fathers and mothers they say: "Do not provoke your children to anger by the way you treat them. Rather, bring them up with the discipline and instruction that comes from the Lord" (Galatians 6:4 NLT).

For children they say: "Obey your parents because you belong to the Lord, for this is the right thing to do" (Galatians 6:1 NLT).

Sometimes achieving these ideals is more of a journey than a destination. We won't arrive overnight. While we need to be honest about the reality of our family situation, we can still strive for the ideal.

Every family will struggle as it tries to follow the template described above. Each member must battle his or her own sinful desires, a spiritual enemy, and the world's system, all of which pull him or her in the opposite direction.

It is important to know that families in the Scriptures had problems, too. They didn't always live up to the ideal presented in the Bible, and they remind us that *every* family is dysfunctional in some way.

Cain killed his brother Abel. After the flood, Noah got drunk. Then his son found him naked and had to cover him up. Abraham lied. He also slept with the family maidservant. Jacob swindled his twin brother Esau out of his birthright. Esau wanted to kill his brother. Joseph's brothers threw him into a hole and later sold him as a slave. David had an affair and had the woman's husband killed. Later his own son led a rebellion against him.

Hopefully these stories make you feel better about your own family experience. Every family has dysfunction, but you can find hope and peace in realizing that all the families listed above, though broken, accomplished great things for God. They were works in progress, and so are we. None of us has reached perfection yet. God is still at work in us and through us.

People who have been following Christ for any length of time will often tell you that they've found life to be tougher since they made the decision to follow him. Things don't necessarily get easier. People who follow hard after God can experience hope and peace while struggling at the same time.

We often want to present a picture perfect Pinterest view of Christianity, but in reality, life is rarely picture perfect. It doesn't always live up to our expectations.

I struggle like everyone else. Life isn't easy. I work two jobs seven days a week to keep our family afloat. I'm in debt and struggle most months to pay all my bills.

As a pastor of care, I spend a good deal of time listening to people dealing with loss, divorce, mental illness, or some other crisis. On occasion, people will take shots at me or criticize me.

I experience difficulties in my marriage from time to time. I struggle to raise my kids. My wife and I have lost 12 family members since we got married.

I still sin and wrestle with my sinful nature. Some days I just want to run to a island and escape it all. The truth is that every follower of Christ will have family problems and challenges. Dr. Wayne Grudem says, "There do not seem to be any convincing verses in Scripture that teach that it is possible for anyone to be completely free of sin in this life." In fact, we find the exact opposite in the Bible. The Scriptures tell us, "Who can say, 'I have cleansed my heart; I am pure and free from sin'?" (Proverbs 20:9 NLT). "Not a single person on earth is always good and never sins" (Ecclesiastes 7:20 NLT).

In the midst of struggle, I choose to keep pressing ahead, even when life is tough. I choose to have hope. I choose to have joy. I choose to love. I choose to keep praying and believing. I choose to keep serving and to do all I can to complete God's call on my life. That is what faith is all about. It is a choice to continue to trust in God and cling to his promises, even in the darkest days.

I can do this, and you can, too, because of what Christ has done for us. He faced trouble in this world and overcame it. We can, too, with the help of the Holy Spirit, who gives us a supernatural perspective and strength that is greater than our circumstances.

So as you aim for the ideal of God's plan for your family, don't be disheartened by the reality of your situation or your family's. Growth takes time. Change takes time. Don't give up. Let love be your goal. Continue to love God and love others. Be patient. God isn't through with you or your family members yet.

Peace with People Different Than You

God's love also breaks down barriers between people groups. His love tears down the walls we put up between race, nationality, and gender. The Apostle Paul wrote, "There is no longer Jew or Gentile, slave or free, male and female. For you are all one in Christ Jesus" (Galatians 3:28 NLT).

God's love doesn't remove the distinctions between men and women or ethnic groups. Rather, in Christ, God's love unites us as one. We are not a melting pot but a salad bowl. We are one people created in God's image with unique attributes. We celebrate both our commonality and our individuality. We celebrate both our unity and diversity.

Race was an issue in the early church just like it is today. The two main distinct people groups in that time were the Jews and Gentiles, and there was hostility between them. Jews didn't associate with Gentiles because they saw them as unclean. Even the Apostle Peter, the main leader of the newly formed church, struggled when it came to including Gentiles into their community of faith. Then God gave him a vision and said to him, "Do not call something unclean if God has made it clean" (Acts 10:15 NLT).

Afterwards, Peter went to the house of a Gentile believer named Cornelius. That was something he wouldn't have done before. He told the people gathered in Cornelius' house, "I see very clearly that God shows no favoritism. In every nation he accepts those who fear him and do what is right" (Acts 10:34-35 NLT). God removed the racial barriers that existed between the two groups.

That is not what Satan wants. Satan wants to divide us based on our race, nationality, and gender. But God wants to bring all who worship him together as one. According to the Scriptures, that is how it will be in heaven. Heaven is filled with people "from every nation and tribe and people and language" (Revelation 7:9 NLT).

We must continue to make sure our churches here on earth reflect that same diversity and unity. Even though the people in heaven have different backgrounds and skin colors, they all sing the same song and worship the same Savior. As the people of God, we should lead by example in promoting peace between various people groups. We do that in the here and now as we prepare for the not yet.

Part 5
FINDING HOPE

Chapter 18

FINDING HOPE THROUGH FAITH

Life is unpredictable outside the Garden. Unexpected things happen. When we experience the unexpected, we can become disillusioned, confused, and hopeless. C.S. Lewis said, "Besides being complicated, reality, in my experience, is usually odd. It is not neat, not obvious, not what you expect."[27]

Reality is odd because this world has been subjected to futility by its Creator after the Fall. "For the creation was subjected to futility, not willingly, but because of him who subjected it" (Romans 8:21 NLT).

There is a curse over our land, so we struggle. We experience pain and loss. We experience confusion and frustration. Worst of all, we experience death. We can't fully see or understand all that is happening in us and around us. In moments like this, it can be easy to lose hope.

When we were expelled from the Garden, we were cut off from another reality, another world. Our eyes are now veiled to that other world, but there is something inside of us that connects with stories about it if we choose to listen. A voice buried deep within tells us they are true. All you see with your physical eyes isn't all there is. There is much more. There are memories from Eden, the other world, laden within us. John Ortberg describes this in his book *The Life You've Always Wanted*:

> Frederick Buechner once wrote that every age has produced fairy tales. Something inside us believes, or wants to believe, that the world as we know it is not the whole story. We long for the reenchantment of reality. We hope that death is not the end, that the universe is something more than an enclosed terrarium. So we keep spinning and repeating stories that hold the promise of another world.
>
> But these stories don't simply demand that another world exists. A common feature of fairy tales is that the enchanted world is not far away. You step into a wardrobe and you're in Narnia. You walk through a forest and stumble on a cottage with seven dwarfs. This other world turns out to be far closer than you thought. In fact, the stories that endure are the ones that most deeply touch this longing inside us.[28]

The Scriptures contain many stories of people having other-world encounters. These stories show us how close the other world is. Before being stoned to death, Stephen looked up to heaven and saw Jesus standing at the right hand of the Father. John saw pearly gates, streets of gold, and the rainbow encircling God's throne while he was exiled on the small island of Patmos. Paul saw the risen Christ in a blinding light from heaven on the road to Damascus. Moses saw the glory of God pass before him while in the wilderness. Isaiah saw the train of God's robe and his mighty six-winged seraphim in the temple.

They all caught glimpses of the other world while still in our world. Most of us won't see that reality while here on earth, but something resonates deep within us and tells us it is true. The other world can only be seen through the eyes of faith. The problem is that our spiritual eyes have been blinded. Our sin, the curse, and our expulsion from the Garden have hampered our vision.

Faith restores that vision. It opens blind eyes, the eyes of your heart. When your spiritual eyes are opened, you can find hope. Faith is a strong conviction of things you can't see yet. It is belief in a God you can't see and a place you can't see, but it's not blind. It is a faith based on verifiable evidence of the things God has done in the past. Faith is trusting in what you can't see because of what you can see. The Scriptures tell us, "Faith shows the reality of what we hope for; it is the evidence of things we cannot see" (Hebrews 11:1 NLT).

By faith you know that God is in control of the future. You understand that he knows the future, will deliver what he promised in the future, and is already there in the future. Because of that you can take daily steps of faith that will increase your hope. As faith increases your hope, hope increases your faith. They are closely connected.

God promises his people, "For I know the plans I have for you [...] They are plans for good and not for disaster, to give you a future and a hope" (Jeremiah 29:11 NLT).

This promise was given specifically to Jewish exiles living in Babylon thousands of years ago. They had been deported from their homeland by the Babylonians after their country was destroyed. Their city and places of worship were in ruin. Their families were torn apart. Their dreams were dashed. They were living without hope. God wanted to remind them that he still had plans for them, even though things looked hopeless. God kept his promise. He brought them back to their homeland 70 years later in 537 B.C.

Like the Jewish exiles, we are not home yet. Things in this foreign land often look hopeless. We must look forward to a future and a hope in a Promised Land that lies within the other world. Our hope is that God will lead us home just as he led the Jewish people. We can look to the past and see how God kept his promises to the Israelites, trusting that he will keep his promises to us, too. We gain hope for the future as we look back.

Faith is Understanding This World isn't Your Home

Abraham may be the most famous person of all when it comes to having faith. His faith is recognized by Christians, Jews, and Muslims around the world. He is considered the father of faith in all those religions. His faith has impacted all of us in some way or another, whether we realize it or not.

It all started when God asked him to leave his home and head to another land. The Scriptures say, "It was by faith that Abraham obeyed when God called him to leave home and go to another land that God would give him as his inheritance. He went without knowing where he was going" (Hebrews 11:8 NLT).

Faith is a journey. You don't know all the details that lie ahead. You may not know day by day where God is going to lead you or what he will ask you to do. You have to trust God as you move forward to provide, guide, and lead you to your final destination.

That is what Abraham did. God promised him that he would be a father to many people and that he would be given a new homeland. Abraham believed God. So without a GPS or Google maps he left his homeland and set out for a new land he had never seen. God was his GPS. Abraham was able to set out by faith because he had caught a glimpse of what was yet to come. Something eternal. God was leading him to the land of Canaan, but Abraham had received a picture of another land, a heavenly land. He was looking forward to a place in a world yet to come. "Abraham was confidently looking forward to a city with eternal foundations, a city designed and built by God" (Hebrews 11:10 NLT).

C.S. Lewis wrote about the eternal desire we have in our hearts. He wrote, "If we find ourselves with a desire that nothing in this world can satisfy, the most probable explanation is that we were made for another world."

The things of this world will leave us empty. Like a bucket full of holes, temporal things will not satisfy our desires. Your deepest desires can only be filled by things that are eternal. The Scriptures say, "Yet God has made everything beautiful for its own time. He has planted eternity in the human heart, but even so, people cannot see the whole scope of God's work from beginning to end" (Ecclesiastes 3:11 NLT). The longing for eternity and immortality in your heart was placed there by God.

One of the eternal things you have been longing for whether you realize it or not is your eternal home. You were created for a different home than the one you currently have in this world. A better home. An eternal home with God. This life here is not all there is. It is but a vapor compared to the eternal life God has promised you. What is 70 plus years here on this earth compared to 70 billion plus years in eternity?

Like Abraham, when you live by faith, you look forward to this *eternal home*, a city with eternal foundations built by God, a heavenly homeland. It is a real, physical place with people, cities, animals, and waterfalls. Most importantly, God is at the center of it all. This other world is much like ours but without the problems and pain that exist here. It is paradise.

You may have heard someone say you can be "so heavenly minded that you are no earthly good." Abraham proved there could be nothing further from the truth. Like Abraham, we must be heavenly minded to be any earthly good.

C.S. Lewis said this:

> A continual looking forward to the eternal world is not (as some modern people think) a form of escapism or wishful thinking, but one of the things a Christian is meant to do.

> It does not mean that we are to leave the present world as it is.

> If you read history you will find that the Christians who did most for the present world were just those who thought most of the next.

> The Apostles themselves, who set on foot the conversion of the Roman Empire, the great men who built up the Middle Ages, the English Evangelicals who abolished the Slave Trade, all left their mark on Earth, precisely because their minds were occupied with Heaven.

> It is since Christians have largely ceased to think of the other world that they have become so ineffective in this.

Aim at Heaven and you will get earth 'thrown in':
aim at earth and you will get neither.[33]

When you embrace the truth that your decisions and actions have
eternal implications, you will have a greater sense of urgency in this
temporary world. You will place a greater priority on living out your
calling. You will accomplish greater things in this life. You are but
a traveler passing through this world, a foreigner in a strange land.
That perspective changes the decisions you make today and directly
impacts how you will spend your eternity.

You are going to face opposition along the way on this journey of
faith to your eternal home. The battles you face will be real. Some
will be fierce. You will win some and lose others. Whatever happens,
know that the final battle has already been won. The victory and
your homeland are already secured.

When you get to your eternal home, you will realize how the pain,
disappointments, and struggles all fit together. Live in light of that
eternal perspective while you go through life now.

People who maintain an eternal perspective accomplish great things
in the here and now. Moses led God's people out of slavery from the
greatest nation on earth at that time. He watched God do incredible
things through his life, splitting the Red Sea, providing food from
heaven for an entire nation of people in the wilderness. Though
Moses never got to enter the Promised Land on earth, he looked
forward to the eternal Promised Land.

The Bible is filled with stories of ordinary people like you and
me accomplishing extraordinary things. "By faith these people
overthrew kingdoms, ruled with justice, and received what God
had promised them. They shut the mouths of lions, quenched the
flames of fire, and escaped death by the edge of the sword. Their

weakness was turned to strength. They became strong in battle and put whole armies to flight" (Hebrews 11:33-34 NLT).

They were able to accomplish these things because they kept the eternal in the forefront of their minds. The story doesn't end with them. It continues today. Thousands upon thousands of broken people living in a broken world are finding hope through faith, faith in the eternal things God has promised to his people. They are bringing this message of hope to others, too.

They are all making a difference in the here and now because of their faith in the not yet. God wants you to be included in the list of heroes of the faith. There is only one you. You have a unique calling, gifting, and mission to complete that no one else can. Paul couldn't do the work of Moses. David couldn't do the work of Esther. They each had unique callings and opportunities to live out their faith in an out-of-control world. You do, too.

You might not have to leave your current job. You might be called to stay and live out your faith where you are now. You must simply do whatever God has called YOU to do. If you grasp the eternal truth that this world is not your home, God can show you your individual calling and help you accomplish great things.

Faith is Expressed Through Action

That is what Abel did. Abel was the son of Adam and Eve. He didn't get to live in the Garden with his parents. He didn't get to walk with God in the cool of the day as his father had. He didn't get to eat from the tree of life. He didn't get to see the Garden of Eden, but his father must have told him stories about it. Even though Abel never got to see and experience the Garden for himself, he believed it was a real place. His faith prompted him to action.

The Scriptures say, "It was by faith that Abel brought a more acceptable offering to God than Cain did. Abel's offering gave evidence that he was a righteous man, and God showed his approval of his gifts. Although Abel is long dead, he still speaks to us by his example of faith" (Hebrews 11:4 NLT). Abel's faith was expressed through action. He gave what he could see to a God he couldn't see. The offerings he gave cost him something. They were sacrificial and provided visible evidence of his faith in an invisible God.

It is one thing to say you have faith, but it is another thing to express your faith through what you do. For example, you could say you have faith that a person could walk across a tightrope over the Grand Canyon. It is another thing entirely to walk across it yourself. Faith trusts enough to step out onto the rope and walk across to the other side. Faith is expressed through action. The Apostle James writes, "What good is it, dear brothers and sisters, if you say you have faith but don't show it by your actions? Can that kind of faith save anyone?" (James 2:14 NLT).

Able and his brother Cain were opposites. Cain didn't have the faith his brother had. They grew up in the same home with the same parents but chose different paths in life. They may have shared the same physical DNA, but their spiritual DNA was as different as night and day.

The Scriptures tell us, "The Lord accepted Abel and his gift, but he did not accept Cain and his gift. This made Cain very angry, and he looked dejected" (Genesis 4:4b-5 NLT). Instead of responding in faith to God's correction, Cain became angry. He faced a crisis of belief. God told him what he needed to do. "Sin is crouching at the door, eager to control you. But you must subdue it and be its master" (Genesis 4:7b NLT).

Sin and anger were threatening to subdue Cain like a wild beast preparing to pounce on its prey. He had the power to subdue it, but he didn't. Instead of controlling it, he let it control him. Once sin pounced, it overpowered him.

Cain's anger grew toward God and his brother. He began to have thoughts of murder and came up with a plan. He lured his brother out into a field and killed him. It was cold-blooded, premeditated murder, and it was the first of many to bring hurt and pain to our world.

Afterwards, God confronted him about his crime. "Where is your brother? Where is Abel?" (Genesis 4:9a NLT). Cain was unrepentant. He shrugged off his brotherly responsibility. His sin had caused him to lose his reverence for God, and he answered him with a snarky tone. "I don't know," Cain responded. "Am I my brother's guardian?" (Genesis 4:9b NLT). God could have executed Cain immediately for his crime and irreverence. Instead, he sentenced him to roam the earth as a wandering fugitive (Genesis 4:12 NLT).

Cain made Abel the first martyr of faith. The world often responds with hate, violence, and murder to faith-filled people, expressing its anger against God by persecuting those who believe in him. The people of the world can't kill God, but they can kill those who speak on his behalf. Abel's life and sacrifice is a reminder that faith requires action and that those actions often involve risk. Those who live by faith believe those risks are worth it because of the hope they have for what lies on the other side.

Faith is Believing When You Can't See

Then there is Enoch. There isn't a lot we know about him from the Scriptures. Christian and Jewish traditions say he was the "recipient of special revelations about the spirit-world and the ages to come."[29]

We are told that God was pleased with him because of his faith. He had faith in a spirit-world he couldn't see. He had faith about things that would happen in the ages to come. He believed in what he couldn't see and trusted in what was yet to come.

Enoch's faith pleased God. The writer of Hebrews says that in order to please God, we must have faith. "And it is impossible to please God without faith. Anyone who wants to come to him must believe that God exists and that he rewards those who sincerely seek him" (Hebrews 11:6 NLT). We must believe in the two things we can't see, God and the rewards God promises to those who seek him.

While it is impossible to please God without faith, it is important to know that God accepts you as you are. He doesn't ask you to change yourself before you come to him. Instead he invites you, through faith, to allow him to change you into the person he wants you to be. We are justified by faith alone and not by works. Works become the natural byproduct of our faith.

It doesn't take an enormous amount of faith to please God either. According to God, faith as small as a mustard seed can move mountains. One person who had that kind of faith was Enoch.

God was pleased with Enoch's faith, so pleased that he took him to heaven directly. The Scriptures tell us, "It was by faith that Enoch was taken up to heaven without dying—he disappeared, because God took him" (Hebrews 11:5 NLT).

It was an abduction of the best kind. He was taken directly from this world to the other world. He was here one moment and gone the next. He believed in a place he couldn't see and in a God he couldn't see. When he arrived in heaven, his faith was realized.

The same is true for all of us. While faith involves believing in what you can't see now, one day you will see it. And while you probably won't experience exactly what Enoch did, you will be transported from this world to the next at the moment of death.

Few people have this kind of faith. The people of Enoch's day didn't. Instead of living by faith, they chose to follow their own ways, so the world continued to spin out of control. Violence increased throughout the earth. Everyone looked out for themselves. It was a me-first generation very similar to ours.

The Scriptures tell us how bad things got. "The Lord observed the extent of human wickedness on the earth, and he saw that everything they thought or imagined was consistently and totally evil. So the Lord was sorry he had ever made them and put them on the earth. It broke his heart. And the Lord said, 'I will wipe this human race I have created from the face of the earth. Yes, and I will destroy every living thing—all the people, the large animals, the small animals that scurry along the ground, and even the birds of the sky. I am sorry I ever made them' (Genesis 6:5-7 NLT).

God looked at what our sin had done to the world and regretted making us. It was a sad situation. He hates the out-of-control things in our world more than we do, but that's what happens when people follow their own ways instead of his. Things were so bad that God decided to start over. He chose one man and his family to begin again. The man he chose was Noah.

Faith is Taking on God-Sized Assignments

God came to Noah and warned him that he was going to destroy all the living creatures on the earth through a flood. He asked Noah to build an ark in order to save his family and the animals. God would send pairs of animals to the boat before the flood came.

This was a God-sized assignment. According to the *ESV Study Bible*, "In modern measurements, the ark would have been around 450 feet (140 m) long, 75 feet (23 m) wide, and 45 feet (14 m) high, yielding a displacement of about 43,000 tons (about 39 million kg). The inside capacity would have been 1.4 million cubic feet (39,644 cubic m), with an approximate total deck area of 95,700 square feet (8,891 square m)."[30] That is a big boat! Noah would have to construct all of this without the help of others or modern equipment. He was on his own. This was more than a weekend project. It is possible that it took Noah 100 years to complete.

Noah responded in faith to God's invitation to build the ark. The Scriptures tell us he obeyed God. (Hebrews 11:7 NLT) He started construction. He took the first step. Noah believed what God told him about future events and responded with action in the here and now.

If God calls to you to take on a God-sized assignment, you might experience what Henry Blackaby calls a "crisis of belief." Blackaby says, "You will quickly realize you cannot do what He is asking on your own. If God doesn't help you, you will fail. This is the crisis of belief when you must decide whether to believe God for what He wants to do through you. At this point many people decide not to follow what they sense God is leading them to do. The way you respond at this turning point will determine whether you become involved with God in something God-sized that only He can do or whether you will continue to go your own way and miss what He has purposed for your life."[31]

The choice is up to you. God will let you turn and go your own way if you choose, but he won't give up on you. He stands at the door and knocks. He wants you to experience him and life to the fullest.

Noah must have worked six days a week on this project for many years. He might have started at daybreak and finished at sunset. He probably hit his thumb with a hammer more than once. He might have felt like giving up along the way. He probably wondered if he would ever finish when things looked bleak. The call to build the ark probably didn't make sense at times. His neighbors probably ridiculed him. But he chose to stay focused on what God had asked him to do. You can, too! Noah built the ark in spite of criticism, weariness, and the magnitude of the assignment. His faith allowed the human race and the animal kingdom to live on.

You may not be called to build an ark, but you may be called to build a business, start a ministry, or write a book. Doing what you believe God has called you to do often takes time. It could take many years. People may question or criticize you along the way. They may not understand what you are doing because they can't see what you have seen through the eyes of faith. Like Noah, you must keep moving ahead in faith and do what God has called you to do. No matter how big the assignment is, if God called you to it, he will see you through it. You are not alone. God is with you. And he will work through you as you trust in him.

Faith is Persevering When Things Get Tough

Taking on God-sized assignments means you must persevere when things get tough. Faith doesn't wait for perfect conditions. "Farmers who wait for perfect weather never plant. If they watch every cloud, they never harvest. Just as you cannot understand the path of the wind or the mystery of a tiny baby growing in its mother's womb, so you cannot understand the activity of God, who does all things. Plant your seed in the morning and keep busy all afternoon, for you don't know if profit will come from one activity or another—or maybe both" (Ecclesiastes 11:4-7 NLT).

Faith is moving forward in spite of the possibility that things could go wrong. Faith works hard. It trusts that God sees everything and rewards everything even though others may not see your faith. Faith doesn't demand assurance of success before it begins a project. Faith takes on assignments that are difficult and important, assignments that require boldness. Faith takes risks, does its best, and leave the results to God.

John and Betty Arnold have that kind of faith. They are a husband and wife team who moved to Burkina Faso, Africa, to bring the hope of the gospel. They help build wells to provide clean water for those in need, partner with a local orphanage, and help disabled men and women in the country's capital city. They also coordinate short-term mission trips for teams from the United States. They mentor new missionaries and plug them into local opportunities.

Betty told me, "Life in general is not easy, but we have not been promised easy. But a life lived in obedience to God's will is a life lived fully and wonderfully indeed. I am very much an 'American' girl. I love the United States. I love to shop and eating in restaurants. My husband and I are both very close to our families. I miss my family, my children, grandchildren, parents, extended family and friends very much while living in Africa. In our first bush home we killed 57 poisonous snakes, killed 12 scorpions, and found 37 bats. But I would rather live in Africa, obedient to God's call, far away from my home, family, culture and conveniences, than to be out of God's will. The best place to be for all of us is in the center of God's will."[5] John and Betty have persevered through a lot of tough situations to stay in the center of God's will.

Rocks and Rafts

To persevere in tough times, you have to keep your focus on where you want to go. I learned this lesson when I was in my early twenties.

[5] You can read more about John and Betty's life in Burkina Faso in her book *Adventures in Burkina*

I went on a white water rafting trip with some friends down the Nantahala River in North Carolina. The Nantahala offers Class II-III rapids that are mild but exciting.

We thought we were going on a guided white water rafting trip, but when we arrived at the top of the river to launch along with several other groups, the guided tour company realized that they were short a guide. They asked me if I would be willing to guide my group's raft down the river and told me they would give me some instructions beforehand. I was a little apprehensive at first, but I decided it sounded like a fun adventure and agreed.

The guide who helped prepare me that day told me something that I will never forget. His instructions about guiding the raft down the river had broader implications than just river navigation. He explained that one of the important things I needed to do was avoid the big rocks. I agreed; that sounded like a good plan. Rocks get you stuck. Rocks knock people from the raft into the frigid water. Rocks turn your raft around and send you down the river backwards. That isn't a good thing. You want to avoid the big rocks!

He said the mistake most people make is getting fixated on a big rock in their path when they see it. Instead of looking where they want to go, they focus on where they don't want to go, straight toward the rock. When they do this, they eventually end up guiding the raft directly into it. He explained that in order to avoid the big rocks, you should look at where you want to go and aim for that instead of the rock. When you do, he explained, you will avoid impact and pass safely down the river to your destination. He was right. I guided the raft and its passengers safely down the river that day. The lesson of fixing your eyes on where you want to go instead of where you don't want to go applies to many other areas of life.

If you focus on the obstacles in your path, their bigness, and their scariness, you will most likely hit them head on. You will get stuck on them or thrown off course. Those obstacles will slow you down and may even throw you into the cold waters of life. You must keep your eyes focused on where you want to go, despite the obstacles. You must keep your eyes focused on Jesus. The writer of Hebrews said, "We do this by keeping our eyes on Jesus, the champion who initiates and perfects our faith" (Hebrews 12:2a NLT).

The Christian journey requires endurance, and endurance comes from keeping your eyes focused on Jesus, especially when life gets tough. Look to Jesus as your example and remember that he endured the suffering and agony of the cross. He endured hostility from his opponents. He completed his mission despite incredible opposition. When you look to Jesus to guide you through the river of life, you focus on where you want to go and who you want to emulate. By doing this rather than focusing on your opposition or troubles, you can avoid getting stuck and thrown off course. You can keep moving forward, even when life gets tough. God will show you the path to take and ultimately guide you to your destination.

Faith Disciplines Your Emotions

Living by faith also requires that you deal with your emotions. Emotions are God-given. God created you with the capacity to feel sadness, anger, joy, and peace. In his humanity, Jesus experienced all of the emotions we feel.

Pay attention to your emotions. Listen to them. Lean into them. Face your fears. Cry your tears. Shout with joy.

Many of us are uncertain how to do this. We have trouble expressing authentic emotion. We take selfies when we are looking and feeling good, but when we are depressed and can't get out of bed, we put our cameras away.

This doesn't mean you should dump all your negative feelings onto Facebook or onto every person who comes your way. People may avoid you if you do that. But you do need to be honest with yourself about what you are feeling. Don't be afraid to listen to your heart and discover what is going on inside of you.

We tend to want to shy away in fear from the dark nights of our soul. We don't want to go there, but sometimes we should. Emotions are better dealt with head on. Instead of pushing them down or pretending they're not there, lean into them. Pay attention to them. Grieve when you need to grieve. Laugh when you need to laugh.

Emotions are your heart and soul's dashboard. They reveal what is going on under the hood. Emotions can signal that something needs to be investigated. They can make you aware of a problem or prompt you to take a necessary action. God often uses your emotions to get your attention.

For example, when you get angry and yell at your kids for a minor offense, your anger is acting as a "check engine" light, prompting you to pause and look under the hood. You may realize that your anger sprang from an incident with your boss at work and that you need to apologize to your children and then address the issue with your boss.

Anger, like other emotions, is completely normal and often healthy. It alerts you to your negative feelings and can motivate you to find solutions to problems. It can lead you to protect someone who's being bullied or rescue someone in danger.

We get angry because God gets angry and we are created in his image. His righteous anger leads him to take action all the time.

Jesus acted in righteous anger when he flipped the tables in the temple, making a statement and driving out the people who had perverted the temple's use. His anger was good and necessary.

If anger isn't dealt with, however, it tends to spin out of control and become destructive. It can hurt you and others and lead to problems at work, in relationships, and elsewhere. It can make you feel out of control, enslaved by its power and unpredictability.

You need to remember that anger is a warning light on your dashboard. Emotions are signals, not the engines driving your life. You are called to live by faith, not by your emotions. At times, that is easier said than done. Hard as it may be, you should strive not to let your emotions control you. Rather, let your faith control your emotions.

You can discipline your anger through faith. Faith disciplines anger by starting with the Scriptures. The Scriptures tell us, "don't sin by letting anger control you" (Ephesians 4:26 NLT). God says you can be angry and NOT sin. It all depends on how you handle your emotion. You can be angry and not sin by expressing your anger assertively and in a timely manner.

Being assertive requires you to be direct. You don't have to be pushy or demanding. Just state what you want clearly. Don't assume the other person can read your mind.

Express your anger in a timely manner, too. Don't suppress or ignore it. It will find a way out. If you bottle it up, it will eventually swell and explode onto someone. When you explode in anger, you say and do things you regret. If your fists are clinched, if tears are streaming down your face, or if you feel like anger is about to take control, take a timeout. Say, "I am too angry to talk right now. Let me cool down before we continue this conversation." Take a break. Go for a walk.

Pray. Then come back later to resolve the issue. If you don't come back to resolve it, it will stay bottled up inside of you. You want to be a conduit, not a container, when it comes to anger.

Sometimes the "check engine" light on your emotional dashboard comes on and you don't know what is causing the problem. You can't put your finger on why you are feeling the way you do. You may need outside help, a diagnostic check. Just as a mechanic can diagnose problems with your car, other people can help you diagnose problems with your heart and mind.

Start by asking the one who made you. Ask God to search you and reveal what is going on. The Psalmist prayed, "Search me, O God, and know my heart; test me and know my anxious thoughts. Point out anything in me that offends you, and lead me along the path of everlasting life" (Psalm 139:23-24 NLT).

Allow God to uncover what is going on inside you. Then you might need to talk a good friend, mentor, or professional counselor. Don't be afraid to ask others for help as you try to diagnose the problem.

Just as a car needs oil changes, your emotions need regular maintenance. In order to stay emotionally healthy and function the way God intended, you must take care of yourself. Basic things like sleep and diet have a big impact on the way you feel. If you binge-watch a program on Netflix into the early hours of the morning and don't get much sleep, you will probably be irritable the next day. If you skip meals because you are too busy to eat, you may not only feel hungry, but also be short-tempered with others. How you take care of yourself physically affects how you feel emotionally. Some maintenance is as simple as getting enough sleep and eating right.

Remember, emotions are shifting sand. Once identified, they can be subjected to faith and disciplined by it. If they aren't, they will take control of your life. As C.S. Lewis wrote, "The governor for the sandy shore of our moods is the virtue of faith. Faith disciplines our emotions and teaches them 'where they get off.'"[32]

Faith is Trusting in God Even if Things Don't Go as You Hope They Will

Trusting God is easier in times when things go as we hope they will. A friend of ours, Hope Garvin, was diagnosed with stage four colon cancer. I arranged for the elders of our church to join me as we prayed for her healing. We all had faith that God could heal Hope. After we prayed, she continued to seek healing by undergoing surgery and chemotherapy. Hope is now cancer-free! She has been in remission for the past several years and is doing well. God answered our prayers!

But not every person we pray for gets healed. They may have the same faith and trust the same God, but they experience different outcomes. Many who live by faith don't get healed of cancer. Many who live by faith experience loss, difficulties, or mistreatment. Sometimes, even when you have faith, things don't go the way you'd hoped they would.

Things like this have happened throughout history to people who live by faith. "Some were jeered at, and their backs were cut open with whips. Others were chained in prisons. Some died by stoning, some were sawed in half, and others were killed with the sword. Some went about wearing skins of sheep and goats, destitute and oppressed and mistreated" (Hebrews 11:36-37 NLT).

Faith requires you to trust God even when things go "wrong." Trust that your story will have a happy ending but recognize that it may not happen until you get to heaven. Fix your eyes on the eternal and understand that the ultimate reward for living a life of faith will be realized in the world to come.

Regan Boatner

Randy and Kristin Boatner have a faith like this. They have been friends of ours for a long time, and for a long time, they were unable to have children. They prayed in faith, asking for a child. Other friends prayed along with them.

After eight years of waiting, God answered their prayers. Kristin found out she was pregnant! Her pregnancy would be difficult, but nine months later, they welcomed Regan, a beautiful baby girl, into the world.

One day, Kristin noticed something yellowish reflecting back light in the pupil of Regan's eye. She took Regan to see a retinal specialist when she was 7 weeks old. A couple of days later, the doctor told them Regan had Retinoblastoma (RB), a rare cancer of the retina, in both eyes. Upon further testing, they found out that the cancer had spread to her brain. Her prognosis was not good, and her situation was extremely rare.

Regan underwent 6 months of chemotherapy. Afterward, she had to have her left eye removed and received a surgically implanted prosthetic eye in its place. She was also given hearing aids to account for damage done by the chemo.

When Regan was 2, the doctors told Randy and Kristin that the tumor was back and bigger than before. They could do surgery, but it would only help relieve the pressure; it wouldn't save her life. There was nothing else they could do.

I prayed for baby Regan. She was Randy and Kristin's only child, the child they had waited and prayed for. She was their hope for the future. I prayed that God would heal their little girl. So did many others. I believed God still performed miracles, and I felt that he would perform one for Regan.

God didn't answer our prayers the way we had hoped he would. He didn't heal Regan the way I had thought he would. Regan was taken to a children's hospital to live out the final days of her young life.

Randy and Kristin asked me to come in and pray with them on the last night. Regan lay on the bed with her eyes closed. She had tubes in her body and medical equipment surrounding her. I laid hands on her and prayed. Her parents prayed with me. I hugged Randy and Kristin and left the room to give them privacy during their final moments with their little girl. When I was out of their presence, I broke down and cried for them and for Regan. She died not long after I left.

In the lobby of the hospital, on the way out, a family member stopped me and asked a difficult question. He said, "Why would God take this little girl from loving parents when there are so many kids that are healthy and given to parents who are not loving?" I didn't have an answer. It just didn't make sense.

I struggled with my faith during the next several days. I really didn't understand how God could get glory from letting a little child suffer and die after so many prayers had been offered up for her healing. I didn't understand why we hadn't gotten what we'd hoped and asked for in prayer.

God slowly began to remind me that this world is not the end. Regan hadn't received all the things God promised to her here, but she did receive them in her eternal home. Regan was alive and healed, just not in the way we had hoped. She was healed in heaven.

None of us will receive all that God has promised in this world. We get down payments here and now guaranteeing what is yet to come, but the complete fulfillment of those promises will come later. C.S. Lewis said, "There are far, far better things ahead than any we leave behind."[34]

Chapter 19

THE SOVEREIGNTY OF GOD

We don't always understand the ways or the plans of God. The fact that God allows Satan, other people, and things like cancer to harm us can be troubling. That is one of the reasons I believe people often question God's goodness or even his very existence. If you believe that God is good and all-powerful, then you understand that he has the power to prevent bad things from coming into our world and into our lives. So you might wonder, why doesn't he do something? Why doesn't he cure cancer? Why doesn't he stop all the evil?

God could stop every evil decision and evil choice. But he loved us enough to give us freedom. If we are going to have real freedom, then there has to be the potential for bad things to happen. God isn't taken by surprise by anything. He has had a plan all along. He is in control of this seemingly out-of-control world. God is sovereign.

We need to remember that, in the beginning, God did place us in a world where no bad things ever happened. He didn't want us to eat from the tree that would bring about pain, suffering, and death. He warned Adam and Eve. But they chose to ignore his warning and eat from the tree anyway. He gave them free will, and they chose to go their own way. Now we are experiencing the consequences of their choice. We no longer live in the safety and security of the Garden of Eden. We chose to open Pandora's Box. God didn't create this mess; we did. We broke the world and ourselves. God is not to blame.

It is impossible to reconcile God's sovereignty and human responsibility in our limited understanding and perspective. God tells us, "My thoughts are nothing like your thoughts. And my ways are far beyond anything you could imagine. For just as the heavens are higher than the earth, so my ways are higher than your ways and my thoughts higher than your thoughts" (Isaiah 55:8-9 NLT).

Trying to comprehend God's sovereignty is like trying to comprehend the size of our universe. The Hubble Space Telescope captured the farthest-ever view of the universe. Every day for 10 years it took pictures of one patch of the sky called eXtreme Deep Field. That photo revealed thousands of galaxies billions of light-years away.[35]

The picture revealed that the universe is much bigger than we realized. It is more complex than we can imagine. It is far too great for our finite minds to comprehend. But trying to comprehend the sovereignty of God is even more mind boggling. If the universe is this large and overwhelming, how much more is the One who created it all?

He has all control, all jurisdiction, and all authority over the entire universe. He is the Most High. He is the Supreme Power. Yet, he is still concerned about the details of your life....what you do for a living, where you live, who you marry, etc.

And he wants to walk personally with you through the valleys and mountaintops. He wants to be your shepherd. He wants to bring you to rest in green pastures. He wants to lead you beside peaceful streams. He wants to renew your strength. He will guide you along right paths if you let him. He is close beside you, and he will comfort you on your journey. That is all part of his sovereignty.

God Causes All Things to Work Together for Good

The sovereignty of God also means that he "makes everything work out according to his plan" (Ephesians 1:11b NLT). That is his sovereign will. His will cannot be frustrated, even when bad things happen. His sovereignty allows him to take the bad things in our world and make them work together for good.

"And we know that God causes everything to work together for the good of those who love God and are called according to his purpose for them" (Romans 8:28 NLT).

God can take the hurtful actions of others, the unwarranted attacks of Satan, and any unwanted circumstances that come your way and bring good out of them. He is the only one who can do that. There is no one like him.

This is what enables people like Christopher Sparkman to have hope. By his sovereignty, God took the sinful actions of a gunman and brought good out of them. He also brought something beautiful out of my brother-in-law Randy's grief.

After Randy's wife Sharon died, he met Karen. Karen's husband had passed away not long after Sharon. Randy and Karen were the same age. They had both been married 24 years. It was apparent that God had been involved in the details of their meeting. I had the honor of officiating their wedding a couple of years ago. They have been a blessing to each other and to us. We will always love Sharon and miss her dearly. She has a special place in our hearts. But we love Karen and her two sons now, too. We see what happened as God bringing good out of a bad situation.

God's sovereignty is also what enables people like Randy and Kristin to have hope. Randy and Kristin, like everyone who has ever lost a loved one, will never "get over" it. Grief becomes a part of your life and part of who you are when tragedy strikes you. The hole in your heart will remain until you are reunited with your loved one in heaven. Despite this, Randy and Kristin have chosen not to let grief win. They take many opportunities to reach out to others and show them the love of God. They now serve as foster parents, taking care of kids who don't have a home or family. God is using them to bless the lives of others.

You may not see the good come about quickly. You may have to weather a season of unfair treatment, unwanted circumstances, and undesirable outcomes. But that season will pass just as sure as spring will come after winter.

Joseph

That was true for Joseph in the Old Testament. The winter seasons of his life were long and painful. He was sold by his brothers to slave traders and taken to a foreign land. He was falsely accused of a crime, thrown into prison, and forgotten for many years.

Then spring came.

He went from prison to the palace, promoted from prisoner to prime minister. In his new position of authority, he came face to face with the brothers who had hurt him and changed the course of his life.

He told them, "You intended to harm me, but God intended it all for good. He brought me to this position so I could save the lives of many people" (Genesis 50:20 NLT). That same verse hung above Christopher Sparkman's hospital bed.

Instead of harboring bitterness, Joseph opened his eyes to God's perspective. He came to understand that God loves to display his sovereign power by restoring things that are beyond repair and seemingly unfixable. He transforms the old into something new. He turns defeat into victory. He finds the lost and brings them home. He picks up the shattered pieces and creates a masterpiece. He takes unfulfilled dreams and gives new visions.

When you grasp ahold of this, you will find hope and comfort in an out-of-control world. If you have experienced hurt, loss, or disappointment, you can trust that God can bring good out of it. It may or may not happen in this world, but it will definitely happen in the world to come. God wants you to embrace that promise.

A.W. Tozer said, "While it looks like things are out of control, behind the scenes there is a God who hasn't surrendered His authority."[36] He is behind the scenes working all things together for our good and his glory.

Still, it is OK to ask God questions in difficult times. He wants us to come to him and have honest conversations. He may not answer all of our "Why?"s, but he always wants us to lean into him. Many of the questions we ask may not get answered this side of eternity. We must trust God when he doesn't explain the things we want to know. Since he created us, and all the world around us, he knows what he is doing. We can always trust that God is good, powerful, and eternally in control, even when it doesn't seem like it.

This gives us hope because we don't have to figure it all out; we just have to trust. God is in control of all things, all people, and every circumstance you encounter. And the future he has in store for those who trust him is better than anything we can imagine now.

Part 6
LOOKING
FORWARD

Chapter 20
LOOKING FORWARD TO HEAVEN

Looking Forward to Heaven

If you are a follower of Jesus, you have much to look forward to. What's ahead is greater than anything you could ever leave behind in this world. That should give you hope as you look forward to the time when all things will be brought under control.

The Apostle Paul said, "No, dear brothers and sisters, I have not achieved it, but I focus on this one thing: Forgetting the past and looking forward to what lies ahead, I press on to reach the end of the race and receive the heavenly prize for which God, through Christ Jesus, is calling us" (Philippians 3:13-14 NLT).

Perhaps we don't talk about heaven much because it seems too far away, too mystical, or too unbelievable. Maybe we feel there are too many pressing matters in the here and now. Perhaps we are indeed too earthly-minded. But as the Apostle Paul said, we should constantly be looking forward to what lies ahead in heaven.

Heaven is a real physical *place*. It is the place where God's presence and glory is fully seen, known, and experienced. It is the place to which

Jesus ascended. It is the place that is being prepared for us by him. Jesus wanted this place to be a source of comfort to us as we anticipate what is yet to come. He said, "Don't let your hearts be troubled. Trust in God, and trust also in me. There is more than enough room in my Father's home. If this were not so, would I have told you that I am going to prepare a place for you?" (John 14:1-2 NLT).

The Apostle John was given a vision of this place. "I saw a throne in heaven and someone sitting on it. The one sitting on the throne was as brilliant as gemstones—like jasper and carnelian. And the glow of an emerald circled his throne like a rainbow. Twenty-four thrones surrounded him, and twenty-four elders sat on them. They were all clothed in white and had gold crowns on their heads. From the throne came flashes of lightning and the rumble of thunder. And in front of the throne were seven torches with burning flames. This is the sevenfold Spirit of God. In front of the throne was a shiny sea of glass, sparkling like crystal" (Revelation 4:2b-6 NLT).

Heaven is not a mystical, immaterial place but a physical place full of physical things. There is a throne. There are people. They wear clothes and crowns. There is lightning and thunder. There is fire. There is glass.

The most incredible thing about heaven is that God is at the center of it all. He is sitting on his throne, in control of all things. In heaven, we will see and experience his splendor, majesty, and power without hindrance. It will be an awe-inspiring sight. The people in heaven will respond to who he is in worship, declaring, "You are worthy, our Lord and God, to receive glory and honor and power, for you created all things, and by your will they were created and have their being" (Revelation 4:11 NLT).

When we enter heaven, we will no longer need faith because we will see him with our own eyes, and seeing him will create in us a sense of wonder, fear, and awe unlike anything we have ever experienced on earth. That is the main reason we look forward to heaven. We long to enjoy the beauty of our Creator, to worship him, to experience the peace of his rule.

We will see our loved ones who also trusted Jesus for salvation. We will see those who went to heaven before us. We will see the place where rust and moth no longer destroy and, most importantly, we will see a world completely under control.

While God sits enthroned at its center, heaven is not a never-ending church service. There are things to do, places to explore, and work to be done. Heaven is a vast country, full of indescribably beautiful landscapes. There will be people and parties and celebrations. We will enjoy each other and our Creator. We have so much to look forward to, and that is why we should think about heaven often.

Keeping heaven in mind will prevent you from going down paths that lead you away from your goal. It will help you prioritize your time and money and battle against sinful desires. It can, will, and should motivate you to keep going, even when you feel like giving up.

Ann Voskamp says, "In Christ, you're a native of heaven right now. You aren't a citizen of here trying to work into heaven. You're a citizen of heaven trying to work through here."[37] You have to keep that in mind. You a foreigner in a foreign land, a heavenly diplomat, and an authorized messenger of the Kingdom. The Most High has called you, equipped you, and empowered you to do his work as you journey through this life toward your homeland.

Heaven is your home, and your soul aches to be there. Sometimes experiences of family, familiarity, and love give you a foretaste of what heaven will be like

I loved going to my grandmother's house when I was growing up. There was always good food to eat. There was a big yard to play in. There was a garden where we could pick fresh vegetables. People were nice to each other. Time seemed to stand still while we were there. The troubles of the world would fade away as I sat down at the kitchen table with family for a meal of fried chicken, homemade mashed potatoes, and sweet tea, followed by the best chocolate cake I've ever eaten. It felt like home.

Those memories help build my anticipation for what my true home in heaven will be like.

Heaven is completely curse-free. In heaven, you will be freed from the effects of sin. The Apostle Paul said, "For we long for our bodies to be released from sin and suffering" (Romans 8:23 NLT). You will no longer experience the pain that the curse has brought into your life. You will be more productive without its weight.

The Apostle Paul said, "What shall we say about such wonderful things as these? If God is for us, who can ever be against us?" (Romans 8:31 NLT). While we may experience things on earth that cause us to question whether God is really on our side, heaven will forever settle our doubts. God is for you. He wants the best for you and always has.

What Happens When We Die?

When you die, your soul will continue to live. It will go to one of two places until the final judgment of God.

If you have trusted in Christ for salvation, then your soul will immediately go to heaven when you die. Jesus wanted us to know that. He turned to the thief on the cross next to him before he died and said, "I assure you, today you will be with me in paradise"

(Luke 23:43 NLT). Today that man is in heaven. There was no waiting. There was no purgatory, soul sleep, or state of unawareness. He was immediately taken to heaven when he died. You will be, too, if you have placed your faith in Christ.

In heaven, we will know and recognize each other. After a time of hugs and reunions, we will pick up where we left off on earth. If we were married on earth, we will not be married in heaven. While there is no marriage in heaven, we may be best friends with our spouses. We will see how our marriage on earth pointed us to the relationship between Christ and his church. We will be content and satisfied as we are united with our heavenly bridegroom, Jesus.

If you have not trusted in Christ for salvation, then God will not force you into heaven. He leaves the choice up to you, allowing you to reject his offer of love. People who reject God's salvation will go immediately to hell when they die. There they will await final judgment.

For those who enter hell, the chaos experienced in this life is only the beginning. Hell is a real, physical place where things will forever be out of control. It is a place filled with torment, brokenness, and regret. It is a place "where the maggots never die and the fire never goes out" (Mark 9:48 NLT).

Jesus made sure to warn us about this place. He told a story about a rich man who lived a life of self-indulgence on earth, disregarding the poor. When he died, he went to hell. The poor man who sat outside his gate went to heaven. The rich man was in agony in hell's flames. He asked the poor man to come dip his finger in water and cool his tongue. The poor man couldn't. No one from heaven can cross over into hell. Jesus said, "There is a great chasm separating us. No one can cross over to you from here, and no one can cross over to us from there" (Luke 16:26 NLT). The fate of those in hell is irreversible.

There is no hope in hell for salvation or a second chance. Neither is there reincarnation. The Scriptures say that "each person is destined to die once and after that comes judgment" (Hebrews 9:27 NLT). Hell is final.

Those who reject the grace of God in this life and the salvation that Jesus offers will have to stand and give an account of their lives before God. They will stand before him guilty for their rebellion and sin. No matter how "good" they think they may be, the Bible is very clear that no one is without sin. We all are active participants in the rebellion against God's rule. The difference between people in heaven and people in hell is that those in heaven trusted Christ to forgive them for their rebellion while those in hell rejected the forgiveness Christ offered.

The decisions you make in this life have eternal repercussions. That should be a sobering thought. God wants you to clearly understand that the choices you make today and each day truly matter.

Hell is a temporary holding place for people who refused the offer of salvation. One day the people in hell will face judgment in resurrected bodies. Anyone whose name is not found in the book of life on the day of judgment will be thrown forever into the lake of fire, along with hell and death (Revelation 21:11-15).

A Word About Suicide

People often ask me if people who take their own lives will go to heaven or hell. Before I answer that, I want you to know that I have known people personally who committed suicide. I have done funerals for them and spoken to their families about the questions they have. What I know from these experiences is that for those who committed suicide, the weight of life had become unbearable. They saw no way out. In some cases, they were struggling with depression or some other mental illness.

It is important to know that even people who have followed God can end up taking their own lives. Matthew Warren, the son of Rick and Kay Warren, died of a self-inflicted gunshot wound. Rick Warren is the pastor of Saddleback Church in California and author of the best-selling book *The Purpose Driven Life*. He is one of the most well-known pastors in the world. Yet his son, Matthew, was apparently plagued by pain he was simply unable to scale.

Here is part of the message that Rick Warren sent out to his congregation after his son's death. "In spite of America's best doctors, meds, counselors, and prayers for healing, the torture of mental illness never subsided... after a fun evening together with Kay and me, in a momentary wave of despair at his home, he took his own life."

Matthew is not alone. A news channel reported that, "More than 90 percent of people who kill themselves have a diagnosable mental disorder, most commonly a depressive disorder or a substance abuse disorder."[38]

We read of godly men in the Scriptures who went through seasons in which they wanted to die. Not long after Elijah experienced God sending fire from heaven to perform a great miracle, he said, "I have had enough, Lord. Take my life, for I am no better than my ancestors who have already died" (1 Kings 19:4 NLT).

Then there was Jonah. After God relented and had mercy on the people of Nineveh, the prophet said, "Death is certainly better than living like this!" (Jonah 4:8 NLT).

Neither of these examples justify suicide or make it right, but they reveal the reality that people, even godly people, can reach points at which they no longer want to live. Tragically, suicide for some seems like the only option.

There are many factors that can lead to someone taking his or her own life, but nowhere in Scripture is suicide listed as an unforgivable sin. If a person has placed his or her faith in Christ for salvation, all his or her past, present, and future sins (including the sin of suicide) have been completely forgiven. Based on what I understand about salvation, he or she will go to heaven.

While suicide isn't an unforgivable sin, its consequences are devastating. It hurts those who are left behind the most, plaguing them with questions that can never be answered this side of heaven. The agony they endure does not go away because they are always left wondering why. Those who are left behind must try to pick up the pieces of their lives. Their pain and scars do not heal easily or quickly.

We need to remember that suicide is a permanent solution to a temporary problem. By committing suicide, a person forfeits God's plan for his or her life here on earth. In no way does God ever condone such an act. We were created in his image, and suicide tramples on that image.

We have this hope and promise written by the Apostle Paul: "And I am convinced that nothing can ever separate us from God's love. Neither death nor life, neither angels nor demons, neither our fears for today nor our worries about tomorrow—not even the powers of hell can separate us from God's love" (Romans 8:38 NLT). This verse gives us hope that we will never be cut off from God's love. No person, spiritual being, or sin can keep us from heaven if we have trusted Jesus to forgive us of our sins.

Heaven is an Intermediate Place

While we should look forward to heaven, we also need to know that its current state is not our final destination. Randy Alcorn says, "When a Christian dies, he or she enters into what theologians call the intermediate state, a transitional period between our past lives on Earth and our future resurrection to life on the New Earth. Usually when we refer to "Heaven," we mean the place that Christians go when they die. When we tell our children "Grandma's now in Heaven," we're referring to the intermediate Heaven."[39]

The intermediate heaven is not purgatory; it's still heaven. It just isn't our final destination. In heaven, we are home because God is with us, and he will be with us forever. But there is more to the story. Heaven in its current state will be relocated. One day in the future we will make our permanent dwelling on a renewed earth. In that day we will receive new, resurrected bodies.

Chapter 21

LOOKING FORWARD TO THE RETURN OF CHRIST AND NEW BODIES

Our bodies long to be resurrected because, in their current state, they are weak and susceptible to disease and death. They need to be transformed and made new. There is a great deal of debate about when this will happen. Some believe it will happen in a secret rapture before the Great Tribulation. Some believe it will happen at the Great Tribulation's end. Regardless of when it happens, we can rest assured that someday Jesus will return and give us new, resurrected bodies like his that will never die. Jesus' return and the resurrection of God's people should be the pinnacle of our hope. It is one of the main reasons we can look forward to the future with hope and anticipation.

The Apostle Paul wrote to one of the early churches to remind them of this. They were losing hope as their friends and family died. They wondered about the resurrection of the dead. He reassured them, "For the Lord himself will come down from heaven with a commanding shout, with the voice of the archangel, and with the trumpet call of God. First, the believers who have died will rise from their graves. Then, together with them, we who are still alive and remain on the earth will be caught up in the clouds to meet the Lord in the air. Then we will be with the Lord forever" (1 Thessalonians 4:16-17 NLT).

The Scriptures tell us that "no one knows the day or hour when these things will happen, not even the angels in heaven or the Son himself. Only the Father knows" (Mark 13:32 NLT). Even Jesus doesn't know the day he will return. There are signs we can watch for that must be fulfilled before his return, but we don't know the day or hour. So be wary of anyone who claims to have found some secret code or formula revealing the exact date of Christ's return. If Jesus doesn't know when he will return, you can be assured that these "prophets" don't know either.

When he does return, those who are already in heaven and those who are still on earth will receive immortal bodies. The bodies of the people on earth will be transformed in the blink of an eye. Then the souls of people in heaven will be clothed with their new bodies. On that day, our salvation will be complete.

What will our resurrected bodies be like? The Apostle Paul says, "It is the same way with the resurrection of the dead. Our earthly bodies are planted in the ground when we die, but they will be raised to live forever. Our bodies are buried in brokenness, but they will be raised in glory. They are buried in weakness, but they will be raised in strength. They are buried as natural human bodies, but they will be raised as spiritual bodies. For just as there are natural bodies, there are also spiritual bodies" (I Corinthians 15:42-44 NLT).

Our spiritual bodies will not be subject to sickness or disease. Cancer, heart disease, and all other illnesses that have affected our mortal bodies in this age will no longer affect us. There won't be any ambulances, hospitals, doctors, or nurses because they will no longer be needed. Arthritis, allergies, and head colds will be forever eradicated. Our imperishable bodies won't age or wrinkle. Male pattern baldness will be a thing of the past. Our new bodies will always maintain their youthful vitality and appearance.

When we receive our new bodies, death will finally be defeated. "When the perishable has been clothed with the imperishable, and the mortal with immortality, then the saying that is written will come true: "Death is swallowed up in victory. O death, where is your victory? O death, where is your sting?" (I Corinthians 15:54-55 NLT).

Our spiritual bodies will never die. The curse of death that was unleashed when Adam and Eve ate from the tree of knowledge of good and evil will forever be removed.

There will be continuity between our current bodies and our new spiritual bodies. Maybe we will have the same hair color, the same eyes, the same nose. But our new bodies will also be different, possessing immortal qualities. Our spiritual bodies will be raised in glory just as Jesus' body was raised in glory.

One of the features of Jesus' glorified body was its glow. The Scriptures tell us, "His face was like the sun in all its brilliance" (Revelation 1:16 NLT). We can assume that our bodies will be beautiful and radiant, too.

We see an example of this in the life of Moses. As Moses spent time with God alone on the mountain, his face began to glow with brightness. It radiated God's glory. Our new, resurrected, spiritual bodies may also possess brightness. We were created in the image of our Creator, who is clothed in light, and we will reflect his light.

Our new bodies will also have power that our current bodies do not. Maybe you will be able to run a marathon without growing weary. Maybe you will be able to climb a mountain without breaking a sweat. Our spiritual bodies won't tire from work or play like our current bodies. We will be able to do things that we cannot do in our mortal bodies.

Since we have this to look forward to, we have hope. We know that whatever sacrifices we make in this life for God's Kingdom will not be made in vain. We can give ourselves fully to God's work because, whatever loss we experience in this life, we will be rewarded with new bodies when Christ returns.

The Final Judgment

In the end, God will settle all accounts, making all things right. He will judge all the people who ever lived. He will even judge the angels who rebelled against him.

On that day, our accuser, Satan, will be "thrown into the lake of fire and sulfur where the beast and the false prophet were, and they will be tormented day and night forever and ever" (Revelation 20:10 NLT). This lake of fire was prepared specifically as the place of punishment for Satan and his angels. Satan will be vanquished there forever. He will no longer be able to tempt us or accuse us or, to kill, steal, and destroy the good things in our lives and our world.

God will also judge all the people who ever lived. All of us will stand before the resurrected Christ in resurrected bodies and receive judgement determining our eternal destiny.

"And I saw a great white throne and the one sitting on it. The earth and sky fled from his presence, but they found no place to hide. I saw the dead, both great and small, standing before God's throne.

And the books were opened, including the Book of Life. And the dead were judged according to what they had done, as recorded in the books. The sea gave up its dead, and death and the grave gave up their dead. And all were judged according to their deeds. Then death and the grave were thrown into the lake of fire. This lake of fire is the second death. And anyone whose name was not found recorded in the Book of Life was thrown into the lake of fire" (Revelation 20:11-15 NLT).

Eternal punishment like this may seem too harsh to imagine, but maybe our perspective is skewed. Maybe we have done such a good job embracing the grace of God that we have neglected to think on the judgment of God. His holiness and justice require that he call the world to account for its rebellion. He must judge sin. There is no escaping that truth. I imagine we will have a greater appreciation for his grace and mercy in light of his judgment.

The final judgment of God will display his righteousness and holiness while also demonstrating his grace and mercy. We will clearly understand that the judgment of a holy, perfect, and loving God is a good thing. For all the times we thought things weren't fair on earth, God's final judgment will settle everything. God will deliver fairness and justice to all. We will look on and declare that all of God's judgments are right, true, and good.

The judgment of God will forever demonstrate that he is in control. God will make all things right. He will allow those who refused his love and grace to have their wish and be far from him. He will welcome those who received his grace and forgiveness into his eternal rest on the new earth.

Chapter 22

LOOKING FORWARD TO A NEW HEAVEN AND NEW EARTH

Eden will be restored, and God will create a new heaven and a new earth in which we will live forever. "Then I saw a new heaven and a new earth, for the old heaven and the old earth had disappeared. And the sea was also gone" (Revelation 21:1 NLT).

God may not create this new heaven and earth out of nothing the way he did in the beginning of time. Rather, he will make something new out of something old, renewing the universe. There will be continuity between the new and old, but none of the bad things that plagued us in the old will have a place in the new. All of creation will live in harmony forever.

> That day the wolf and the lamb will live together;
> the leopard will lie down with the baby goat.
>
> The calf and the yearling will be safe with the lion,
> and a little child will lead them all.

The cow will graze near the bear. The cub and the calf will lie down together. The lion will eat hay like a cow.

The baby will play safely near the hole of a cobra. Yes, a little child will put its hand in a nest of deadly snakes without harm.

Nothing will hurt or destroy in all my holy mountain, for as the waters fill the sea, so the earth will be filled with people who know the Lord.

(Isaiah 11:6-9 NLT)

Randy Alcorn challenges us to imagine what this will be like.

So wake up. Imagine this world in its original condition. The happy dog with the wagging tail, not the snarling beast, beaten and limping and starved. The flowers unwilted, the grass undying, the blue sky without pollution. People smiling and joyful, not angry, depressed, and empty. The Curse will be reversed: this is the promise of God (Revelation 22:3). Take it to the bank.

With the Lord we love and with the friends we cherish, believers will embark together on the ultimate adventure, in a spectacular new universe awaiting our exploration and dominion. Jesus will be the cosmic center. Joy will be the air we breathe.

And right when we think "it doesn't get any better than this"—it will.[40]

We will live with God forever in resurrected bodies that will never die. We will live in a world where moth and rust don't destroy, where natural disasters, hunger, and pain are distant memories. The curse will be forever removed, and we will experience the fullness of eternal life.

The longing you have now for eternity was put into your heart by God. The frustration of living in a world out of control is knowing something isn't quite right, that there is something more you're missing. When you enter the new earth, however, you will gain a new perspective, and the eternity in your heart will be realized. You will still learn and grow, and you will continue to depend on God as you enjoy fresh understandings.

You will never grow tired of worshiping God, nor run out of things to worship him for. In addition to this, you will never have to worry that sin may once again throw things out of control.

The heavenly city that Jesus prepared for us will be established on the new earth. "And I saw the holy city, the new Jerusalem, coming down from God out of heaven like a bride beautifully dressed for her husband" (Revelation 21:2 NLT). The city will be made of pure gold with walls of jasper. It will have 12 pearl gates and a river of life-giving water flowing down the center of the main street. We will once again have access to the tree of life from which we were banished in the Garden. All of creation will be redeemed. The earth, the animals, and the people will all work together in perfect harmony for all eternity.

Looking Forward to God at the Center of Our World

If you pause to think about the current state of our world, it's obvious that something isn't right. There is a darkness in our land. Listen to the news and it won't take you long to realize that something is missing. There is a void where God's dwelling on earth should be. We live in a world without God at the center.

His presence is not fully known or understood now. The light of his glory does not shine with its full strength. When the new heaven and earth are established, God will once again be at the center of our existence, giving light and life. We will no longer need the light of the sun or moon because his glory will shine in the holy city.

"And the city has no need of sun or moon, for the glory of God illuminates the city, and the Lamb is its light. The nations will walk in its light, and the kings of the world will enter the city in all their glory" (Revelation 21:23-24 NLT). All the nations and world leaders will walk in the light of Jesus. With Jesus reigning as the Prince of Peace, true world peace will finally exist.

There will be a new way of life in the new world with God at the center. Death will be no more. Mourning will be a thing of the past. Crying will be long forgotten. Pain will be but a distant memory. "He will wipe every tear from their eyes. There will be no more death or mourning or crying or pain, for the old order of things has passed away"(Revelation 21:4 NLT).

There will never be any more brokenness or chaos. This is the dream that is hidden in your heart. The longings you have had to be freed from the chaos of our world and to experience lasting peace and contentment will be realized.

The lyrics from the *Song Don't You Want to Thank Someone* by Andrew Peterson capture the hope of the new world that is coming:

> And when the world is new again
> And the children of the King are ancient in their
> youth again

> Maybe it's a better thing
> A better thing
> To be more than merely innocent
> But to be broken then redeemed by love. [6]

This is the final act in the great story of redemption for which we are waiting. God will triumph over evil, Satan, and man's sin, bringing all things under control. God, in his sovereignty, will bring history to its ultimate conclusion and renew all that is wrong in this world.

A world *under control* is coming. The Kingdom of God is working its way through our world as you read. It will continue its progress until all is made new. Jesus and the Holy Spirit call out to us to join them, inviting us to take part in eternal life "The Spirit and the bride say, 'Come.' Let anyone who hears this say, 'Come.' Let anyone who is thirsty come. Let anyone who desires drink freely from the water of life" (Revelation 22:7 NLT).

The final two verses of the Bible sum up the book and our hope. "He who is the faithful witness to all these things says, 'Yes, I am coming soon!' Amen! Come, Lord Jesus! May the grace of the Lord Jesus be with God's holy people" (Revelation 22:20-21 NLT).

---

[6] Andrew Peterson - "Don't You Want to Thank Someone" Lyrics. Artist: Andrew Peterson. Album: Light for the Lost Boy

Bibliography

Intro

1. "FedEx Shooter's Suicide Note: 'I Am a Sociopath. I Want To...'" AJC.com: Atlanta Georgia News, AJC Sports, Atlanta Weather. Web. 24 July 2016.
2. "911 Calls Released From Georgia FedEx Shooting - NBC News." NBC News. Web. 24 July 2016.
3. "Co-worker Gives FedEX Shooting Victim a Fighting Chance." WSBTV. 30 Apr. 2014. Web. 24 July 2016.

Chapter 3

4. "The Weight of Our Story: Light for the Lost Boy by Andrew Peterson." Story Warren. Web. 24 July 2016.

Chapter 6

5. Ortberg, John. The Life You've Always Wanted: Spiritual Disciplines for Ordinary People. Grand Rapids, MI: Zondervan Pub. House, 1997. Kindle Edition, 17.
6. Drake, Bruce. "Number of Christians Rises, But Their Share of World Population Stays Stable." Pew Research Center RSS. 22 Mar. 2013. Web. 25 July 2016.

Chapter 8

7. "Sleep Paralysis Symptoms, Treatment, and Causes." WebMD. WebMD. Web. 25 July 2016.
8. Lucado, Max, Kevin Harney, and Sherry Harney. Before Amen: The Power of a Simple Prayer: Study Guide. Kindle Edition, 75.
9. Forsyth, Peter Taylor. The Soul of Prayer. London: Independent, 1949. Print, 4.
10. ESV Study Bible: English Standard Version. Wheaton, IL: Crossway, 2011. Print, Notes on Genesis 32:28.

Chapter 9

11. Lewis, C. S. The Problem of Pain. New York, NY: HarperOne, 2001. Print, Chapter 6.
12. "ACA Spurs Modest Growth in Spending." Health Care Costs 101: ACA Spurs Modest Growth. Web. 25 July 2016.
13. "Joni Is Interviewed by TIME Magazine." Joni and Friends. Web. 25 July 2016.
14. "Why Joni Eareckson Tada Wants to Bring Her Wheelchair to Heaven." Justin Taylor Why Joni Eareckson Tada Wants to Bring Her Wheelchair to Heaven Comments. Web. 25 July 2016.

Chapter 10

14a. http://www.littlethings.com/grieving-advice-old-man/

Chapter 11

15. Grudem, Wayne. Systematic Theology: An Introduction to Biblical Doctrine. Zondervan. Kindle Edition, 226.
16. "BibleGateway." John 3 NLT. Web. 25 July 2016.

Chapter 12

    17. Rosen, Eliot Jay. Experiencing the Soul: Before Birth, during Life, after Death. Carlsbad, CA: Hay House, 1998. Print.

Chapter 13

    18. "Bounce Your Eyes - New Life." New Life. 02 Aug. 2013. Web. 25 July 2016.

Chapter 15

    19. Grudem, Wayne. Systematic Theology: An Introduction to Biblical Doctrine. Zondervan. Kindle Edition, 788.
    20. ""What Is the Most Hurtful Thing Your Parents Have Said to You?"" What Is The Most Hurtful Thing Your Parents Have Said To You? Web. 25 July 2016.

Chapter 16

    21. "Top 5 Christian Theologians: Karl Barth." Trevin Wax Top 5 Christian Theologians Karl Barth Comments. Web. 25 July 2016.

Chapter 17

    22. Townsend, John. Loving People: How to Love and Be Loved. Thomas Nelson. Kindle Edition. (Kindle Locations 1065-1066).
    23. Townsend, John. Loving People: How to Love and Be Loved. Thomas Nelson. Kindle Edition. (Kindle Locations 1123-1128).
    24. Townsend, John. Loving People: How to Love and Be Loved. Thomas Nelson. Kindle Edition. (Kindle Location 580).

25. "The Slippery Slope - Peacemakers." Peacemakers. Web. 25 July 2016.

26. ESV Study Bible: English Standard Version. Wheaton, IL: Crossway, 2011. Print, Character Types in Proverbs.

Chapter 18

27. Lewis, C. S. Mere Christianity: A Revised and Amplified Edition, with a New Introduction, of the Three Books, Broadcast Talks, Christian Behaviour, and Beyond Personality. San Francisco: HarperSanFrancisco, 2001. Print. 21-22.

28. Ortberg, John. The Life You've Always Wanted: Spiritual Disciplines for Ordinary People. Grand Rapids, MI: Zondervan Pub. House, 1997. Print.

29. F. F. Bruce. The Epistle to the Hebrews. Kindle Edition. (Kindle Location 3226).

30. ESV Study Bible: English Standard Version. Wheaton, IL: Crossway, 2011. Print, Notes on Genesis 6:15.

31. Blackaby, Henry T., and Claude V. King. Experiencing God: How to Live the Full Adventure of Knowing and Doing the Will of God. Nashville, TN: Broadman & Holman, 1994. Print, 134.

32. "Faith Is a Habit." CS Lewis Blog. 17 Sept. 2013. Web. 25 July 2016.

33. "C.S. Lewis Institute." Reflections December 2006-Living in Hope. Web. 25 July 2016.

34. Lewis, C. S., and Walter Hooper. The Collected Letters of C.S. Lewis. San Francisco: HarperSanFrancisco, 2004. Print.

Chapter 19

35. "Hubble Telescope Reveals Deepest View of Universe Ever."
    Space.com. Web. 25 July 2016.
36. "A.W. Tozer- A Man of God." - Timeline. Web. 25 July
    2016.

Chapter 20

37. "When You Feel like You Don't Really Belong." A Holy
    Experience. 02 June 2014. Web. 25 July 2016.
38. "Son of Pastor Rick Warren Commits Suicide." Myfox8com.
    06 Apr. 2013. Web. 25 July 2016.
39. "Intermediate (Present) Heaven vs. Eternal Heaven -
    Resources - Eternal Perspective Ministries." Intermediate
    (Present) Heaven vs. Eternal Heaven - Resources - Eternal
    Perspective Ministries. Web. 25 July 2016.
40. "About Randy Alcorn." Longing for Heaven? Web. 25 July
    2016.

Edwards Brothers Malloy
Thorofare, NJ USA
December 27, 2016